Hardware Malware

Synthesis Lectures on Information Security, Privacy, & Trust

Editors
Elisa Bertino, *Purdue University*
Ravi Sandhu, *University of Texas, San Antonio*

The Synthesis Lectures Series on Information Security, Privacy, and Trust publishes 50- to 100-page publications on topics pertaining to all aspects of the theory and practice of Information Security, Privacy, and Trust. The scope largely follows the purview of premier computer security research journals such as ACM Transactions on Information and System Security, IEEE Transactions on Dependable and Secure Computing and Journal of Cryptology, and premier research conferences, such as ACM CCS, ACM SACMAT, ACM AsiaCCS, ACM CODASPY, IEEE Security and Privacy, IEEE Computer Security Foundations, ACSAC, ESORICS, Crypto, EuroCrypt and AsiaCrypt. In addition to the research topics typically covered in such journals and conferences, the series also solicits lectures on legal, policy, social, business, and economic issues addressed to a technical audience of scientists and engineers. Lectures on significant industry developments by leading practitioners are also solicited.

Hardware Malware
Christian Krieg, Adrian Dabrowski, Heidelinde Hobel, Katharina Krombholz, and Edgar Weippl
2013

Privacy for Location-based Services
Gabriel Ghinita
2013

Enhancing Information Security and Privacy by Combining Biometrics with Cryptography
Sanjay G. Kanade, Dijana Petrovska-Delacrétaz, and Bernadette Dorizzi
2012

Analysis Techniques for Information Security
Anupam Datta, Somesh Jha, Ninghui Li, David Melski, and Thomas Reps
2010

Operating System Security
Trent Jaeger
2008

Hardware Malware

Christian Krieg, Adrian Dabrowski, Heidelinde Hobel, Katharina Krombholz, and Edgar Weippl

ISBN: 978-3-031-01210-5 paperback
ISBN: 978-3-031-02338-5 ebook

DOI 10.1007/978-3-031-02338-5

A Publication in the Springer series
SYNTHESIS LECTURES ON INFORMATION SECURITY, PRIVACY, & TRUST

Lecture #6
Series Editors: Elisa Bertino, *Purdue University*
                Ravi Sandhu, *University of Texas, San Antonio*
Series ISSN
Synthesis Lectures on Information Security, Privacy, & Trust
Print 1945-9742   Electronic 1945-9750

Hardware Malware

Christian Krieg, Adrian Dabrowski, Heidelinde Hobel, Katharina Krombholz, and
Edgar Weippl
Vienna University of Technology and SBA Research

SYNTHESIS LECTURES ON INFORMATION SECURITY, PRIVACY, &
TRUST #6

ABSTRACT

In our digital world, integrated circuits are present in nearly every moment of our daily life. Even when using the coffee machine in the morning, or driving our car to work, we interact with integrated circuits. The increasing spread of information technology in virtually all areas of life in the industrialized world offers a broad range of attack vectors. So far, mainly software-based attacks have been considered and investigated, while hardware-based attacks have attracted comparatively little interest. The design and production process of integrated circuits is mostly decentralized due to financial and logistical reasons. Therefore, a high level of trust has to be established between the parties involved in the hardware development lifecycle. During the complex production chain, malicious attackers can insert non-specified functionality by exploiting untrusted processes and backdoors. This work deals with the ways in which such hidden, non-specified functionality can be introduced into hardware systems. After briefly outlining the development and production process of hardware systems, we systematically describe a new type of threat, the *hardware Trojan*. We provide a historical overview of the development of research activities in this field to show the growing interest of international research in this topic. Current work is considered in more detail. We discuss the components that make up a hardware Trojan as well as the parameters that are relevant for an attack. Furthermore, we describe current approaches for detecting, localizing, and avoiding hardware Trojans to combat them effectively. Moreover, this work develops a comprehensive taxonomy of countermeasures and explains in detail how specific problems are solved. In a final step, we provide an overview of related work and offer an outlook on further research in this field.

KEYWORDS

hardware Trojan, hardware security, logic testing, formal verification, side-channel analysis, hardware Trojan taxonomy, attacker taxonomy, attack taxonomy, countermeasures taxonomy

Contents

List of Figures

CHAPTER 1

Introduction

1.1   MOTIVATION

In our modern world, computer systems are used in nearly all areas of daily life—from starting the day with coffee and the electronic newspaper to driving to work and home again, and cooking dinner. Most devices that we use contain microprocessors, often without the users being aware of it. But it is not only our everyday life that is supported by microprocessors; military and financial applications are principally controlled by microprocessors as well. With the growing number of microprocessors embedded in different types of applications comes an increased threat of vulnerabilities and malicious functionalities at the hardware level.

If we imagine that these microprocessors are defective or even contain deliberately placed malware that makes them remote-controllable and allows unauthorized access, we can picture dire scenarios for the future. In 2010, the motor vehicle manufacturer Toyota had to place one of the biggest product recalls in automobile industry in the U.S. About 6.5 cars were affected due to reports of unintended acceleration. Imagining that such an error can be placed maliciously by an attacker into software and hardware parts highlights the importance for advanced research in hardware and embedded systems security. Checkoway et al. [26] presented attack surfaces in the automotive ecosystem. They highlight the problem of compromised Electronic Control Units (ECUs), which are responsible for parsing channel messages and could be exploited by transmitting malicious input. Another prominent example to picture the threat of malicious hardware is the worm *Stuxnet* that had been detected in 2010. The malicious code was designed specifically to observe and control technical processes in industrial facilities. Due to the high complexity of the worm, it is generally assumed that the designers of Stuxnet had knowledge of unrevealed Microsoft exploits and the architecture the industrial control system of the facility. Supposing that such worm could be (partially) implemented in hardware, the operation could be even more precise. In general, using hardware Trojans to attack infrastructure and military applications, such as industrial complexes and power plants, can have a huge impact on the populations of a region and yield high financial damages. These examples illustrate how pervasive computer hardware has become in human life and how much the society depends on it—without being aware of it.

The same pervasiveness applies to military applications. Tanks that no longer attack the enemy but their own forces, or cruise missiles that hit domestic instead of hostile areas are terrifying examples of the consequences compromised hardware could have.

Previous efforts to address the threat of malicious hardware are limited to academic models and hypotheses. Because of market limitations to only a few domains (such as military applications), there has not been any development of commonly usable solutions for detecting manipulated chips and preventing their malicious insertion.

The awareness of software security in the general population is growing due to popular science literature and media reports. In these scenarios, the malicious functionality is assumed to be in the software, while the hardware is considered as trusted. However, malware in hardware and especially in silicon is an emerging threat and security mechanisms have to be analyzed and improved in order to guarantee a certain level of security and trust in hardware components.

1.2   BACKGROUND

The topic of security in IT primarily deals with risks and threats that originate from malicious software. Frequently mentioned risks include viruses, worms, and Trojan horses.

Fighting such malicious programs often requires them to access resources under the user's control first. These can be routines of the operating system, memory, or processor of a computing system. If a malicious program uses such a resource, it can be detected—roughly speaking—by monitoring a subordinate resource.

A short example to illustrate this: While surfing the Internet, an unwary user allows a program designed to leak user data to be installed. Because this program is running at all times, it can be detected among the running processes. The monitoring of these processes is a function of the operating system and lies one abstraction layer beneath the malicious program. If the operating system itself were to be infected, a different detection and deletion approach with an abstraction layer beneath the operating system would have to be used.

Attackers always try to conduct their attacks as unnoticed as possible. This is the reason why they will try to place their attacks as low in the abstraction levels as possible. This leads to a race of sorts between attackers and defenders to focus attacks and detection methods on the most fundamental functional entities.

For example, King and Chen [44] implement a malicious hypervisor that compromises the security of every virtual machine it manages. There is no way of detecting this attack from within the virtual machines because all functions (including functions of the operating system) are based on the functionality of the hypervisor.

The logical consequence for an attacker is to implement attacks on the lowest possible abstraction layer—the **hardware**.

This book is devoted to the risks resulting from compromised hardware. We aim to systematically examine the vulnerabilities that result from modern development and production processes. Furthermore, we will analyze strategies for avoiding this special form of attack.

1.3   PRODUCTION PROCESS OF HARDWARE SYSTEMS

An attack at hardware level differs fundamentally from an attack at software level. In contrast to software, hardware is a physical good and can only be altered in limited ways after manufacturing.

Hardware also cannot be duplicated as easily as software, as it requires significant effort and human resources.

In order to examine attack scenarios at hardware level, the following questions must be answered.

1. Who are the possible attackers?

2. Where are possible vulnerabilities located?

3. How can vulnerabilities be protected?

To answer these questions, we will first give a brief overview of the production and design process of microprocessors to provide a detailed understanding of the risks and vulnerabilities originating in the hardware production process.

1.3.1 WORKFLOW

Growing competitive pressure and ever shorter product launch times make it necessary to reuse already developed hardware components. Therefore, hardware must be present in a special, reusable

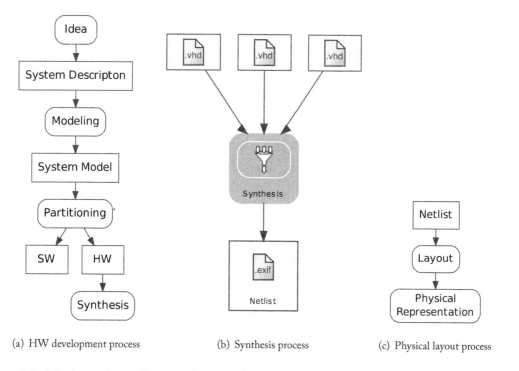

(a) HW development process (b) Synthesis process (c) Physical layout process

Figure 1.1: Hardware design flow, synthesis, and layout process.

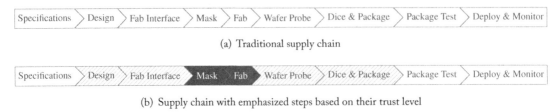

Figure 1.2: Supply chains in IC production proposed by Sharkey [72].

format. The solution is to textually *describe* the *behavior* of the hardware, so that it can be generated through *synthesis*. Such descriptions are verbalized in so-called hardware description languages (*HDL*) such as VHDL or Verilog.

Figure 1.1(a) shows some substantial parts of the hardware development process. After the system has been described in natural language, the system model is designed in a modeling language. Based on the model, partitioning is used to decide which parts of the functionality will be implemented in hardware and which in software. Through synthesis, the hardware will be generated from the system model components intended for this purpose.

Figure 1.1(b) shows how the synthesis process works. The "source code" that is scattered across multiple files is translated into a format that only includes logic gates and connecting signals.

The resulting representation of the hardware *netlist* is then mapped to the desired target technology (ASIC, FPGA). Here, the respective logic elements are placed on the chip and are connected to each other via electrical connections (*place and route*). The result is a file that fits the physical representation of the hardware (see Figure 1.1(c)).

The physical representation is submitted to the chip manufacturer (*Tape Out*). After manufacturing, the chips are returned or delivered to the market.

1.3.2   VULNERABILITIES

As mentioned above, the hardware design and production process consists of many steps and corresponding interfaces. It is easy to see that each of these steps in the process, as well as every transition between the process steps, is vulnerable.

Figure 1.2(a) summarizes every step of the process, focusing on the physical manufacturing process. The neutral background signifies that all of the process steps are trusted. (cf. Sharkey [72], Tehranipoor and Lee [76])

To address the issue that some steps in the design and production process cannot be trusted, they are categorized based on their trustworthiness. Figure 1.2(b) illustrates this by assigning white to the trusted and black to the non-trustworthy steps. If no assumption about the trustworthiness can be made, the step is hatched.

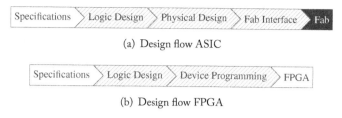

(a) Design flow ASIC

(b) Design flow FPGA

Figure 1.3: Design flow ASIC and FPGA proposed by Sharkey [72].

Sharkey [72] also specifies confidentiality classes for the different development processes for ASICs (Figure 1.3(a)) and FPGAs (Figure 1.3(b)).

The Defense Science Board, Department of Defense, U.S. [30], provides a detailed look at the links between the development and production processes and the risks involved (cf. Figure 1.4).

In this way, malevolent developers can insert malicious functionality into the hardware description directly as code. Furthermore, it is also possible that functionality bought as so-called *IP cores* (*IP—Intellectual Property*) implements malicious, unwanted functionality in addition to the expected functionality. It also cannot be ruled out that errors or additional functionality are introduced by software tools such as synthesizers or place-and-route tools (cf. Chakraborty et al. [25]).

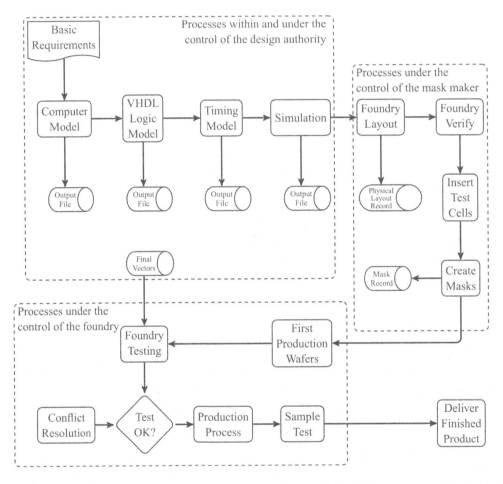

Figure 1.4: Generic design flow proposed by Defense Science Board, Department of Defense, U.S. [30].

CHAPTER 2

Hardware Trojans

Recently published literature provides a comprehensive overview of hardware-based attack vectors. Most of this literature deals with the question how intellectual property can be protected by preventing integrated circuits from being replicated by a competitor. However, in recent years we additionally had to consider external attacks that use vulnerabilities in transmission protocols or test mechanisms in this research area.

An interesting attack vector is the so-called *hardware Trojan* (cf. U.S. Department of Defense [30]), which adds additional, non-specified functionality to the hardware. Hardware is a physical good and therefore, the infection with malicious functionality must take place during the development or production process (see Section 1.3). In this chapter, we surveyed the components, types, and attack parameters of hardware Trojans. Furthermore, we introduce metrics for measuring a hardware Trojan's threat, probability of occurrence, and costs for detection measures.

2.1 COMPONENTS

There are ambiguous classification systems for hardware Trojans. One of the most prominent taxonomies of hardware Trojans component classifications is proposed by Wolff et al. [87], who classify Trojans based on their trigger and payload mechanisms.

Since Trojans can consist of more than two different functional units (i.e., trigger and payload), we propose a general approach that tries to cover all eventualities.

Therefore, we consider a Trojan as a *system*. The system performs specific functions and has a certain number M of *input signals* and a certain number N of *output signals*. Furthermore, the system consists of K *subsystems*, which are connected by signals. *Signals* can be either *internal* or *external*. Internal signals exist between subsystems. External signals are routed out of the entire system.

For the sake of simplicity and comprehension, we will, in the following, use an established description of Trojans by trigger and payload mechanisms as proposed by Chakraborty et al. [20]. We extended their definition by an additional component: Trojans may interact with their environment, so we propose adding a classification of how Trojans communicate with their surroundings. For this reason, we introduce the *interfaces* of a Trojan as a new class of our taxonomy. An overview of our taxonomy is given in Figure 2.1 and is incrementally explained in the following subsections.

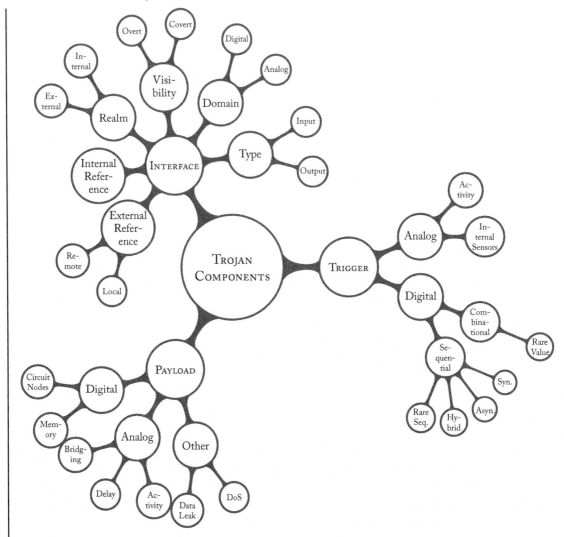

Figure 2.1: Hardware Trojan taxonomy.

2.1.1   TRIGGERS

Triggers have the task of activating the payload mechanism of a hardware Trojan. To avoid detection during functional tests, this is based on rare events such as the passing of 10,000 s presence of a specific bit pattern, or reaching a certain voltage value within the electronic circuit. Activation is also possible via an external radio signal.

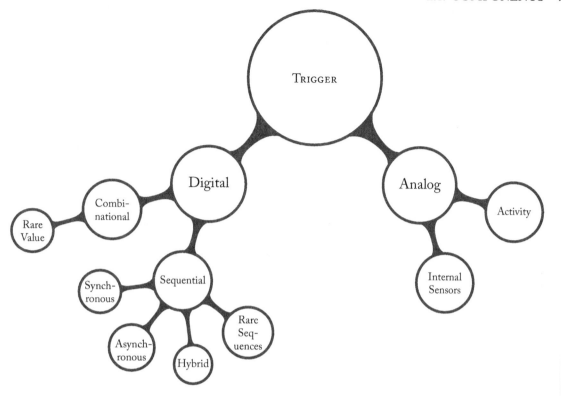

Figure 2.2: Trigger mechanisms to activate a Trojan according to Chakraborty et al. [20].

Figure 2.2 shows the classification of trigger mechanisms as described by Chakraborty et al. [20]. The proposed classes are explained in detail, whereas the branching of the classification is inferable from the figure. We will, therefore, concentrate on the fine granular classes.

Analog Triggers use sensors or the occurrence of a specific physical event, e.g. rising ambient temperature, in order to activate a hidden hardware Trojan and thus can be further classified in Activity and Internal Sensors.

Digital Triggers cover all forms of triggers that are depending on digital signals and can be further classified in Combinatorial and Sequential types.

Combinatorial Triggers are digital triggers that monitor signals of a circuit and trigger if a specific pattern, a *rare value*, is present on this signal (Figure 2.3(a)).

Sequential Triggers are the second digital type of triggers, and comprises memory elements (i.e., flip-flops). *Synchronous* triggers are controlled by a clock (Figure 2.3(b)), *asynchronous* triggers are controlled by any logic signal (Figure 2.3(c)). A *hybrid* trigger is a combination

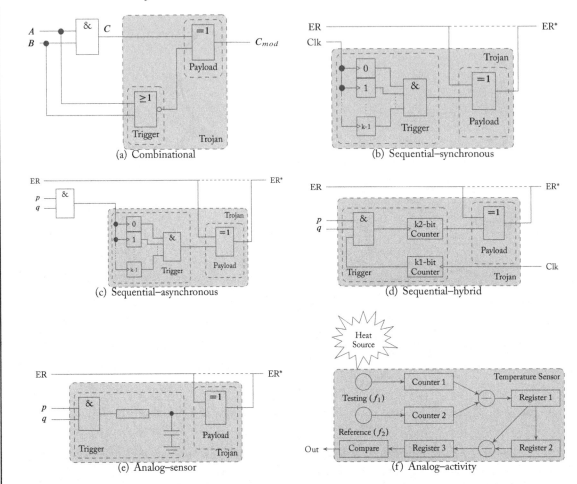

Figure 2.3: Examples of triggers according to Chakraborty et al. [20].

of synchronous and asynchronous triggers (Figure 2.3(d)). Furthermore, sequences of rare events, *rare sequences*, can serve as trigger conditions.

Internal sensors Use simple analog components to serve as trigger (Figure 2.3(e)).

Activity Triggers are of the type of analog trigger that use, e.g., temperature as a measure. If the temperature in a certain part of the circuit exceeds a certain value, the trigger condition is met and the Trojan is activated (Figure 2.3(f)).

2.1.2 PAYLOAD

After activation, the functionality of a hardware Trojan is executed. The possibilities include intercepting passwords, turning off the device, or even destroying it entirely. Figure 2.4 shows the classification of Trojans by their payload mechanisms. According to Chakraborty et al. [20] and Wolff et al. [87], payloads can be divided into digital and analog. We expand this classification with an additional class that includes other types of possible payload options.

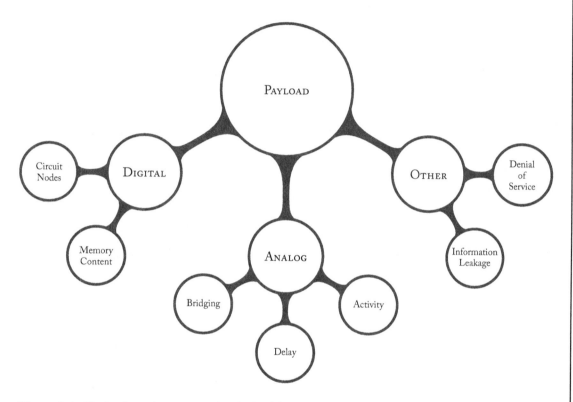

Figure 2.4: Payload mechanisms with which a Trojan can occur according to Chakraborty et al. [20].

Digital Trojans can influence either logical states of internal *circuit nodes* or the content of memory blocks.

Analog Trojans can influence the parameters of a circuit in a way that disturbs the performance, power consumption and noise. Figure 2.5(a) shows a circuit that realizes a *bridging fault* with a resistor over V_{DD}. In Figure 2.5(b), a *delay* is introduced by a capacity to ground. The *activity* in the circuit can also be increased to make it age prematurely.

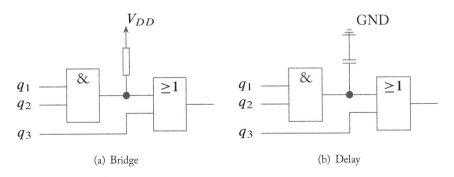

Figure 2.5: Analog payload according to Chakraborty et al. [20].

Other Payload are also possible, for example information leakage (cf. Jin and Makris [38], Lin et al. [52], Tehranipoor and Lee [76]) or a Denial-of-Service (DoS) attack that turns off the functionality of a hardware system (cf. Adee [3]).

2.1.3 INTERFACES

One of the most important components of a Trojan are its connections to its environment, its *interfaces*. Through its interfaces, a Trojan is connected to the outside, allowing the designer of the Trojan to control and communicate with the Trojan. We classify interfaces of Trojans according to the following criteria.

1. The **type** determines whether the interface is an input or output device.

2. The **domain** specifies a digital or analog interface.

3. **Visibility** determines whether the interface operates overtly or covertly.

4. **Internal reference** means that if an interface is an output, the internal reference is to be understood as a source. If it is an input, the internal reference is a sink.

5. **External reference** is the opposite of 4.

6. The **realm** describes whether the interface connects the components of a Trojan (internal), or connects the Trojan to the outside (external).

Figure 2.6 illustrates the proposed classification in more detail. We explain and emphasize the relationship between the illustrated classes based on the following three classes:

Type An *input* provides data to the Trojan. The source of an input can originate either *locally* from the compromised hardware system, or *remotely* from outside the system. An input can lead either to the *trigger* of a Trojan or into the part of the Trojan that implements the payload mechanism. If an input leads to the trigger, it can have the trigger condition applied. If an input leads to the payload part, it can originate from a different part of the Trojan (for example, the trigger). Such an interface is called an *internal* interface. An *external* interface connects the Trojan to signals from other parts of the compromised system. An *output*, in turn, provides data from the Trojan to its surroundings. The source is a component of the Trojan (e.g., *trigger* or *payload*). The sink of the output can either be another component of the Trojan (internal interface), or it can be located locally or remotely (external interface).

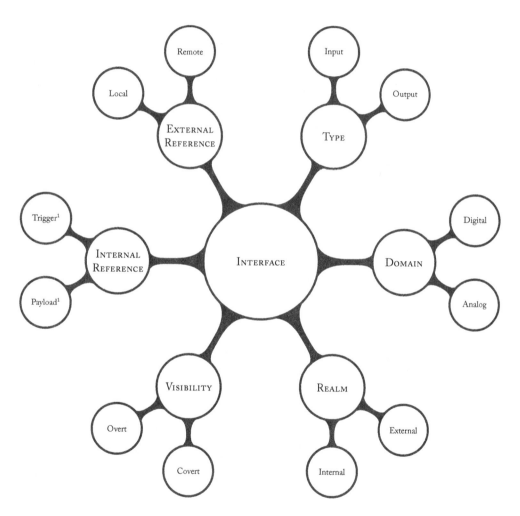

Figure 2.6: Classification of the interfaces of Trojans.

[1] *Trigger* and *Payload* can be viewed as just another interface, however in an functional view, these are major components as shown in Figure 2.1

Visibility In the design of an *overt* interface, no effort is made to hide the signal's existence during operation, e.g., a compromised digital signal that comes directly from the payload of the Trojan and connects to a pin of the IC. Signals that serve as the input of the trigger and can carry the trigger condition fall into this category, as well. A *covert* interface operates on a channel that is not visible without special efforts. Lin et al. [52] present an approach in which the signal of the supply voltage is modulated with payload. The modulation is achieved by Code Division Multiple Access (CDMA). Here, a code is used without which the signal cannot be demodulated and distinguished from noise. To obtain the payload, one must perform a side-channel analysis on the signal of the power supply. In order to influence the supply voltage, large capacitances are charged/discharged. Another example of a covert interface is presented by Jin and Makris [38]. Here, the authors change the transmission signal of a wireless device within the legitimate tolerances depending on the desired signal. A side-channel analysis must be performed on the transmission signal to obtain the payload.

Domain Data with two states that are represented by logic levels is exchanged via a *digital* interface. An *analog* interface allows data exchange in a continuous spectrum of values.

2.2 TYPES

Rad et al. [62] present a comprehensive taxonomy, in which they characterize Trojans based on their properties. Trojans are roughly divided by their physical, activation, and action characteristics. Banga [10] also provided a similar classification with regard to physical properties, activation types and action types.

Physical We divide the physical properties in type, size, and distribution characteristics. The *type* of a Trojan determines whether it is functional or parametric. A *functional* Trojan executes specific functions using specific logic, whereas a *parametric* Trojan changes existing components of an integrated circuit (such as electrical connections or logic). The *size* determines the extent of a Trojan. A *small* Trojan is around the size of a transistor, whereas a *large* Trojan is around the size of a gate or larger functional units (macros). The *distribution* of a Trojan can be either *compact* or *loose*. While the components of a compact Trojan are closely adjacent to each other, loose Trojans are scattered across the entire chip area. Unlike Chakraborty et al. [20], Rad et al. [62] distinguish trigger and payload mechanisms not by domain (digital/analog), but by origin.

Activation The *activation* (the trigger mechanism) can either be always-on or take place due to a trigger condition. The occurrence of a condition can be observed by *sensors* (voltage, temperature, external environmental conditions such as electromagnetic interference, pressure, humidity, etc.). *Logic-based* activation is also possible. Trigger conditions can arise from the *internal state*, by *inputs*, or by *counter* and *clock*. *Inputs* can result from *data*, *commands*, and *interrupts*.

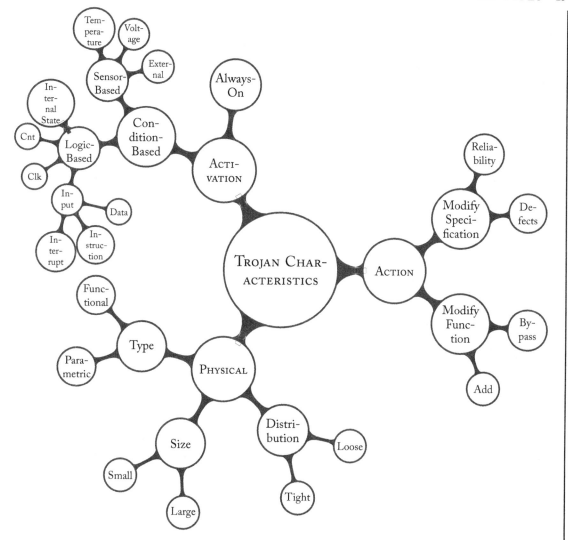

Figure 2.7: Classification of Trojans according to Rad et al. [62].

Action Trojans can also be classified by their *action* characteristics. Either the *function* or the *specification* can be modified. A function can be *added* or *bypassed*. The specification can be modified in such ways as to introduce *defects* to the geometry of the chip, which has a negative impact on the *reliability* of a system.

2.3 ATTACK PARAMETERS

We model hardware Trojans through multiple dimensions in order to keep track of isolated dependencies but also the entire device. All these dependencies influence the characteristics of the Trojan's attack mechanism. Obviously, the Trojan's attack mechanism determines the applicable countermeasure mechanism. For that reason, we emphasize the parameters below for analyzing the Trojan's attack characteristics. We limited ourselves to the following dependencies and discuss them in detail in the next subsections.

Hardware abstraction layer In order to develop effective methods against Trojans, we have to consider at which level the Trojan is operating, and thus model the Trojan's hardware abstraction layer. For example, a side-channel analysis makes no sense if the Trojan was inserted at system level by a malicious designer.

Domain For the sake of simplicity, we emphasize only the selected domain. Therefore, if only the digital domain is investigated, a Trojan in the analog domain could remain hidden.

Target technology Furthermore, we propose that the target technology of the Trojan should be taken into account. For instance, a Trojan in an Application-Specific Integrated Circuit (ASIC) will behave differently than a Trojan in an Field-Programmable Gate Array (FPGA).

Injection phase When developing countermeasures, it is also important to consider the *injection phase* of a Trojan. Based on the entire life cycle of an IC, this can happen during the design or production phases, but also at runtime, for example through manipulation of the bitstream of an FPGA.

Topology A Trojan's topology can appear in many different shapes. For example, it could be distributed across multiple chips, or it could only consist of one gate. By considering this fact, we can also detect Trojans that might otherwise stay hidden.

2.3.1 LEVEL OF ABSTRACTION

Figure 2.8 shows a systematic breakdown of the levels of abstraction. Subclass relationships indicate logical dependencies, while connections with dots denote those interfaces on which verifications between the connected levels can be made.

A crucial interface in the life cycle of an IC is the so-called tape-out. This is the term used for when the final design is sent to the manufacturer. The reason we consider this interface so important is that at this point the responsibility for the IC is transferred from the designer to the manufacturer. The hardware design is implemented and can no longer be altered, at least not without restrictions.

While the levels that are passed before the tape-out offer a multitude of attack vectors, after the tape-out attack vectors are limited to the insertion of additional circuit components and modifications of existing circuit components. Verifying the absence of Trojans can only be done by comparing it against models of the pre-tape-out phase. Current approaches take advantage of the side-channel analysis of already fabricated chips to compare their results with simulation models (cf. Alkabani and Koushanfar [7], Banga and Hsiao [12, 13, 14], Jin and Makris [37], Li and Lach [50], Potkonjak et al. [59], Rad et al. [62], Wang et al. [83], Wolff et al. [87]). It is assumed that the models are free of Trojans. Such models are also called "golden models" in this context (see also Section 3.2.4).

Although the papers cited above provide interesting approaches to the detection of Trojans, they still assume that a Trojan is inserted post-tape-out. Simulation models are usually based on the logic or the circuit level. This is problematic when a Trojan is inserted pre-tape-out since this is part of the simulation model and cannot be detected by side-channel analysis.

Pre-tape-out, Trojans can be inserted at all levels by malicious designers. It is also conceivable that they might be added during the transition from one level to another, for example, by malicious compilation tools (cf. Nelson et al. [57], Potkonjak [58], Roy et al. [68]). The transitions are represented by dots connected by thick lines in Figure 2.8.

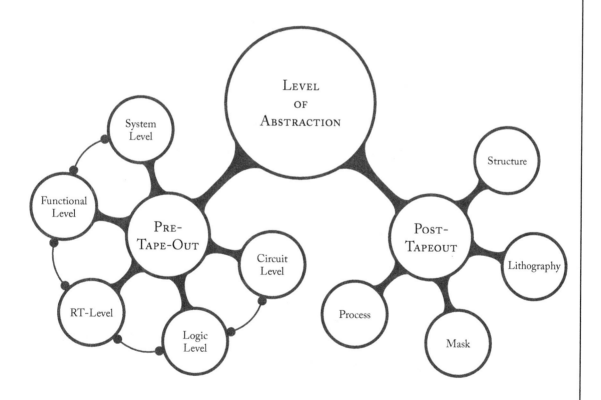

Figure 2.8: Abstraction layers at which Trojans can be realized.

2.3.2   TECHNOLOGY DOMAIN

It is also important to consider the technology domain in which a Trojan is implemented. All components of a Trojan can be implemented in different technology domains. For example, an input signal can be digital and a leaked output signal can be realized in the analog domain. An interesting example of this approach is given by Jin and Makris [38].

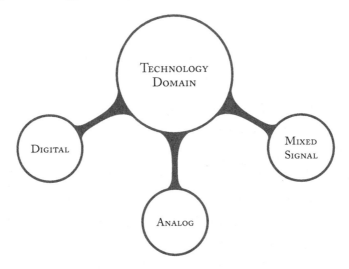

Figure 2.9: Technology domains in which Trojans can be realized.

Figure 2.9 shows the three possibilities: digital, analog, and mixed signal. A *mixed-signal system* is a chip that has both analog and digital components. An analog output signal is not necessarily produced by analog circuit components. For example, temperature differences can be modulated with an output signal. The temperature—an analog signal—can be generated by, e.g., ring oscillators—a digital circuit (cf. Kean et al. [40]).

2.3.3   TARGET TECHNOLOGY

As technology changes, so do future types and characteristics of Trojans. In addition, the possibilities for injection vary immensely. Technology must therefore be taken into consideration when investigating Trojans.

To be able to take into account all the existing technologies in which hardware is realized, a classification is necessary. Figure 2.10 provides a general overview of the seemingly endless variety of opportunities.

Hardware technologies can be generally divided into discrete and integrated circuits. Discrete circuits are electronic devices that are wired on a printed circuit board. *Integrated* circuits are complete circuits that are integrated into one package. Inputs and outputs are connected to connector pins outside of the package and used for wiring with other electronic components. Dis-

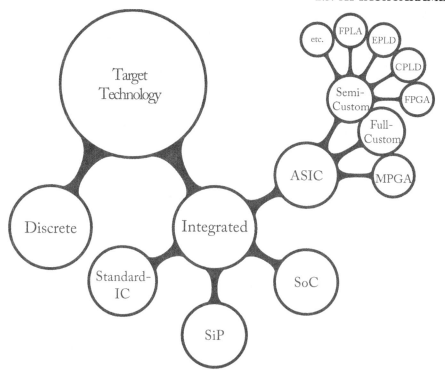

Figure 2.10: Technologies with which Trojans can be realized.

crete circuitry may include integrated circuits, which are divided into more finely granular classes, explained below:

Standard IC Standard ICs are—as the name suggests—components that implement a standard function and can be used in many different applications. Examples include logic gates, operational amplifiers, shift registers, and microprocessors. Standard ICs are produced in very large quantities and are therefore relatively inexpensive.

ASIC ASICs are ICs that are designed for a specific application. As the cost of a specially designed IC is highly dependent on the production quantity, there are various forms of ASICs. *Full-custom* refers to a technology that offers the greatest possible freedom. Here, everything down to the transistor level can be determined. Because all mask sets need to be developed specifically for production, the use of this technology is only viable in very large quantities. Using *standard cells*, finished assemblies such as logic gates, adders, etc., are assembled from a library to form an ASIC. By using finished modules with known electrical and physical properties, the design phase becomes much cheaper compared to a full-custom solution. Another large subset of ASICs are called *semi-custom* solutions. Here, similar types of logic building blocks are prefabricated. The actual function is determined through the internal wiring, which is usually realized with transistors. Some examples of semi-custom devices are FPGA, Complex Programmable Logic Device (CPLD), Electrically Programmable Logic Device (EPLD), and Field-Programmable Logic Array (FPLA).

SoC & SiP Another class of ICs are System-on-a-Chip (SoC) and System-in-a-Package (SiP). SoC are complete computer systems that are housed on a single chip. SiP, on the other hand, consist of several chips that are stacked into a single package.

2.3.4   INJECTION PHASE

The life cycle of a hardware system provides numerous opportunities to include hidden, unwanted functionality. Figure 2.11 illustrates the stages of the life cycle of a digital IC. The life cycle of an IC can be roughly divided into four parts: 1. *design*, 2. *manufacture*, 3. *test*, and 4. *deployment*.

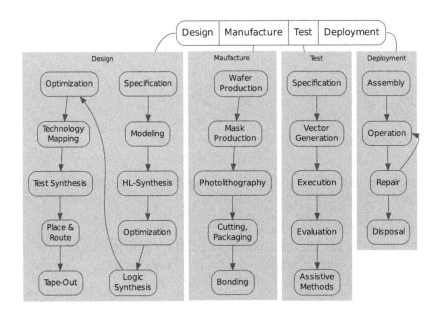

Figure 2.11: Injection phases in which Trojans can be included (for a digital ASIC).

Design phase In this phase, the properties of the system to be developed are specified. After modeling in a system description language, the high-level synthesis is carried out. After performing optimization measures in order to meet different criteria, the behavior of the system is mapped to a structural representation using logic synthesis. Then the design is mapped to the target technology and the circuit components are placed and connected on the chip area. After further optimization, a possible test synthesis takes place, which inserts dedicated logic (like scan flip-flops) and helps test the manufactured system. Finally, the tape-out takes place, i.e., the transfer of the production documents to the manufacturer.

Manufacture phase Subsequently, a mask manufacturer will first produce the masks for the semiconductor production (cf. Defense Science Board, Department of Defense, U.S. [30]). The chip maker uses the masks in a photolithographic process to expose the wafers produced by the wafer manufacturer. Typically, a multitude of identical ICs are produced on a wafer.[1] After the photolithography, the wafer is cut, the individual chips are inserted into packages and the external connections of the ICs are connected to the connection pins of the package (*bonding*).

Testing phase This phase is used to verify the functionality of the produced IC (functional test). The tests are carried out by test engineers. After the tests are specified, test vectors are generated, which are applied to the primary input of the integrated circuit. With the help of the employed dedicated test logic, the outputs of the integrated circuit are monitored. A subsequent analysis of the test results allows making a statement about the proper functioning of the IC. Assistive methods (such as specialized vector generation, side-channel analysis, statistical methods) allow testing for specific aspects (such as the detection of Trojans).

Deployment phase When the test phase is complete and correct functionality of the integrated circuit has been certified, the IC is *deployed*. After the assembly, in which the IC is inserted into its application, operation of the IC follows, which can be interrupted by failures and repair times. When the deployment phase is completed, the disposal of the IC marks the end of its life cycle.

All of the phases in the life cycle of an IC mentioned above are vulnerable to attacks. The attacks differ significantly with the phase in which they occur, as well as by the *attackers* involved.

2.3.5 ATTACKERS

Naturally, the properties of attackers who introduce Trojans cannot be ignored. Attackers can be classified by various properties in the following basic categories:

1. the **phase** in the life cycle of an IC in which the attack is performed;

2. the **function** of the attacker (designer, manufacturer, mask manufacturer, developer of development tools);

3. the **sphere** of the attacker (where they can become active, what their influence is);

4. the **knowledge** of attacker (which information is available);

---

[1]except for Multi Project Wafers (MPW)

5. the **expertise** of the attacker (which skills are available); and

6. the **resources** that are available to attackers (both financial and human)

Figure 2.12 illustrates the relationships.

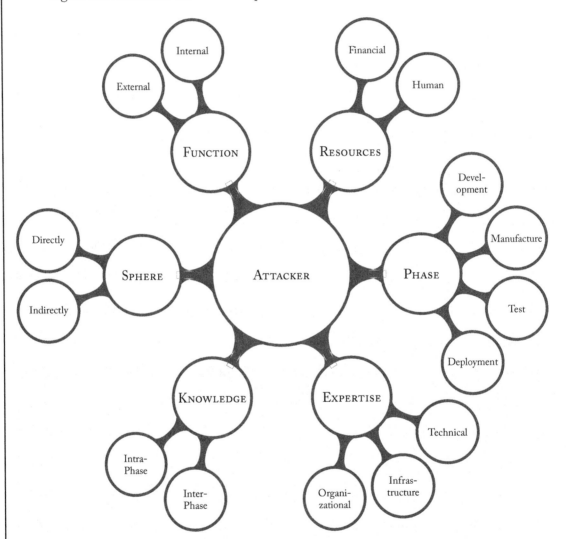

Figure 2.12: Significant properties of an attacker for a Trojan attack.

Baumgarten et al. [17] present a taxonomy of attackers. Here, the supply chain in the production of an IC is of central importance. On this basis, they define the following classes of attackers: *design*, *synthesis*, *fabrication*, and *distribution* attackers. We suggest, however, not using the supply chain as a basis for a taxonomy of attackers, but instead basing it on the life cycle of an IC. Analogously to Baumgarten et al. [17], attackers can, therefore, be divided into *design*, *manufacture*, *test*, and *deployment* attackers.

Ali et al. [5] investigate attacks in which several attackers are involved (see also p. 74). They focus on the knowledge that an attacker needs to successfully carry out an attack. An attack against an AES core is used as an example. The designer of the AES core implements malicious functionality to obtain the secret key. The leakage of the key itself, however, must be done during operation, so an operator needs to know of the existence of the malicious functionality.

Sturton et al. [75] assume that an attacker can carry out an attack in such a way that it remains undetected during functional tests. Here, the attacker gains knowledge of the testing process, as well as about the nature and the generation of the test vectors. Generally, we can also assume that an attacker who studies the functions of the IC during the production phase using reverse engineering will be more successful if she has access to design specifications, which are produced during the design phase. Based on previous considerations, we therefore propose a classification of the attackers' *knowledge* based on phase boundary. If an attacker has knowledge about only one injection phase, we speak of *intra-phase knowledge*. However, if their knowledge extends over several injection phases, we speak of *inter-phase knowledge*.

Kuhn [48] shows an example about optical reverse engineering an integrated circuit. He shows how layer by layer is removed by etching in order to reconstruct the functionality using optical microscope analysis. This requires extensive *technical expertise* and the reverse engineer must also have great *infrastructural expertise* to be able to make a suitable measurement setup and evaluate the results.

For an attack to remain unnoticed during verification (structural verification, formal verification) and tests (functional tests), *organizational expertise* is needed as well. This ensures knowledge about the design and production process as well as the utilized methods and tools.

Function The *function* of an attacker is classified using their relation to the design and production process. If an attacker is directly involved in the development and production process, she can directly and personally influence the resulting system. For example, a malicious designer can add functionality in the form of hardware description code (cf. Alkabani and Koushanfar [6]). Malicious circuits can be injected into unused chip resources by a malicious manufacturer after tape-out (cf. Jha and Jha [36]). Such attackers will be referred to as attackers with *internal* function, as opposed to attackers with *external* function, who have no direct influence on the system during the design and production process. External attackers compromise a system indirectly by attacking general, non-individual structures. An example would be a compromised design tool (cf. Roy et al. [68]), such as a synthesizer. Since the attacker (in this case also the attacker of the development tool) has no knowledge about the system being developed, she has to attack general structures such as flip-flops, gates or the like.

Resources   Another important property of attackers are the *resources* available to them. Attacks will
vary in type and scope depending on the availability of resources. We must distinguish between *financial* and *human* resources. Depending on the type of attack, considerable human
and/or financial resources may be necessary. The estimated probability of a specific attack
can be estimated using threat models. For example, the reverse engineering of technology-
dependent representations (format of the hardware design, which is present in the tape-out
phase) has immensely high personnel costs if the entire design is to be analyzed in reasonable
time. Additional expensive equipment is required that needs adequate funding. In contrast,
the insertion of malicious circuits by a malicious designer during the design process has a
low cost in both personnel and financial terms.

Sphere   The *sphere* of an attacker marks the possibilities of her influence on the life cycle of an IC,
so that an attack can be carried out. *Direct* influence exists if the hardware in question can
be compromised by the attacker without the need for intermediate steps. *Indirect* influence
exists if the hardware can only be attacked via intermediate steps.

2.3.6   TOPOLOGY

Another important aspect in the investigation of Trojans is the way they are arranged in a hardware
system—the *topology*.

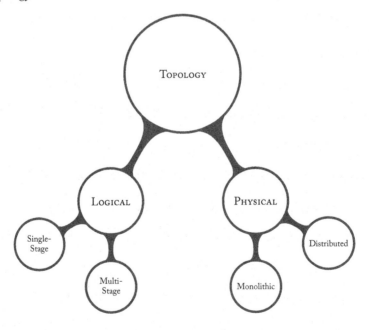

Figure 2.13: Topologies of Trojans.

We must distinguish between logical and physical topology, as illustrated in Figure 2.13.

Logical The *logical* topology defines how the Trojan "works" (i.e., how its function is fulfilled). This can be executed in one or multiple stages. A *multi-stage* Trojan goes through several phases until its function is fulfilled entirely. An example of a multi-stage Trojan is described by King et al. [45]. The authors implement a microprocessor with an embedded hardware Trojan (stage 1), which serves as the basis for further, software-based attacks (stage 2). Jin and Makris [38] implement a compromised Advanced Encryption Standard (AES) core within a wireless transmission device. After the bits of the secret key have been intercepted (stage 1), they are leaked over a covert output channel via manipulation of the wireless transmission signal within the legitimate tolerances (stage 2). A *single-stage* Trojan, however, only has one phase in which its function is executed entirely. Examples of single-stage Trojans are given by Wolff et al. [87].

Physical The *physical* topology defines how the Trojan is physically distributed on the hardware system. If the topology of the Trojan is *monolithic*, the gates and the transistors are arranged in the immediate vicinity. A *distributed* Trojan is spread over the entire hardware system. This could also be the case for a discrete hardware system where the Trojan is allocated across multiple chips. But even within a single IC, the components of a Trojan can be spread across the whole chip area.

2.4   METRICS

Based on the previously introduced components and considerations, in this section we propose metrics that facilitate the estimation of hardware Trojans' attack probabilities. We introduce the *structural complexity* as a metric, describing the functional complexity of the Trojan itself, which is based on the distribution in terms of size and component types. We analyze the effects of a hardware Trojan on the hardware system's temporal and technical supply facilities. Furthermore, we introduce and discuss the attack probability, activation probability, implementation costs, and detection costs.

2.4.1   STRUCTURAL COMPLEXITY

The structural complexity is a significant measure that describes the logical structure of a Trojan. Therefore, for the calculation we consider the amount of logic gates k as well as the amount of storage elements (flip-flops) d, determining the amount of states S that the Trojan can adopt. If the hardware Trojan does not incorporate any storage elements, then the Trojan is implemented through a combinatorial circuit. The amount of possible states is determined by the following Eq. (2.1):

$$S = 2^d .$$
(2.1)

The amount of primary inputs e determines the amount of possible states E for the input vector (cf. Eq. (2.2)):

$$E = 2^e . \tag{2.2}$$

Likewise, the possible amount of output states for A is determined by the available number of primary outputs (cf. Eq. (2.3)):

$$E = 2^a . \tag{2.3}$$

In that regard, we are able to put the calculated numbers into a relation, consisting of the amount of possible states, primary inputs and outputs. For that, we multiply the amount of possible states by the sum of inputs and outputs, and thus obtain a key figure for the logical complexity K_l (cf. Eq. (2.4)):

$$K_l = S * (E + A) . \tag{2.4}$$

We can conclude that the logical complexity indicates the complexity of the circuit's functionality. The input vector is exponentially increasing dependent on the amount of inputs and, likewise, the output vector is dependent on the amount of outputs. Furthermore, the amount of storage elements determines the amount of output vectors for a specific input vector. Hence, the logical complexity is computed by multiplying the amount of possible states by the sum of inputs and outputs.

On the other hand, the structural complexity is mostly determined by the amount of gates only. Additionally, the nesting depth v can also be used as a criterion for the structural complexity of a circuit. The nesting depth describes the number of logical gate levels that have to be passed so that a primary output is affected by a primary input.

2.4.2 IMPACTS

For the assessment of the impacts of a hardware Trojan, we introduce two key figures: the deviation of the runtime behavior influenced by a Trojan as well as the deviation of the power consumption that is increased by the hardware Trojan's execution.

The runtime behavior of a circuit is determined by the sum of the single pass-through times of the circuit's gates. In that regard, a circuit incorporates one or more paths where each path connects an input and an output. The critical path designates the path that has the highest pass-through time. Hence, the critical path determines the maximum frequency that can be used for operating the circuit.

If a hardware Trojan—or some part of it—are located along the critical path, then the additional gates of the Trojan increase the overall pass-through time, and thus the maximal operating frequency decreases. Considering that behavior, an attacker will seek to implement the Trojan outside the critical path in order to avoid a functional test easily revealing the Trojan's injection. Instead of the critical path, the attack will choose a path with a significantly lower pass-through time so that the Trojan will not affect the maximal pass-through time.

In case a Trojan is injected into a circuit, the derivation Δt from the pass-through time of a path t_d is mainly determined by the Trojan's nested depth v. That is due to the fact that a logical signal has to pass through the number of implemented levels, determined by the sum of the pass-through times of the gates T_i. This relation is represented in the following Eq. (2.5):

$$\Delta t = \sum_{i=0}^{v} t_{d,T_i} . \tag{2.5}$$

The larger the number of the nested depth and the pass-through times of the single gates of a Trojan, the larger the impact on the whole circuit.

Another measure for the impact of the Trojan on the whole circuit is the Trojan's part of the power consumption caused by the additional logical gates that constitute the Trojan. Each of the logical gates has to be supplied with current and voltage, resulting in an increased overall power consumption of the circuit.

Hence, the increased power consumption ΔP caused by a Trojan results from the number of injected gates $k + d$ as well as the respective power consumption P_{T_i} of the injected gates T_i. In this regard, we consider both combinatorial (k) and sequential d (or storage elements) gates as relevant for power consumption. The derivation of the power consumption caused by a Trojan is represented in Eq. (2.6):

$$\Delta P = \sum_{i=1}^{k+d} P_{T_i} . \tag{2.6}$$

Concluding, the larger the number of a Trojan's gates, the larger the impact on the overall power consumption of the whole circuit.

2.4.3 ATTACK PROBABILITY

Based on the previously introduced metrics (cf. Sections 2.4.1 and 2.4.2), we will introduce a measure for assessing the probability of an attacker implementing a hardware Trojan in a circuit.

In the following, we will assume that an attacker is obviously trying to avoid the detection of the injected Trojan during a functional test. Thus, the differences measured between an uninfected and an infected circuit have to be as low as possible. We are, therefore, considering a hardware Trojan as potentially inconspicuous, if its effects remain within the limits of manufacturing deviations.

In order to define characteristics that determine the probability of a hardware attack, we make the following assumptions.

1. The number of the Trojan's possible states S_T is relatively small compared to the number of the overall circuit's states S_{total}. As a consequence, we can determine that $S_T \ll S_{total}$.

2. The amount of the gates $g_T = (k_T + d_T)$ incorporated by the Trojan is relatively small compared to the overall circuit's gates $g = (k + d)$. Thus, we determine $g_T \ll g$.

3. The power consumption ΔP of a Trojan is relatively small compared to the overall circuit's power consumption P. Thus, we determine $\Delta P \ll P$.

4. The runtime behavior of the Trojan $t_{d,T}$ influences the runtime performance of the overall circuit t_d to a relatively small degree: $t_{d,T} \ll t_d$.

5. The Trojan's injection costs are technically and economically feasible.

If the conditions above are met, we can assume that the infection of a circuit is effective due to the low detection probability within a functional test. By considering the key figures in a mathematical relation, we can represent the dependencies in the following Eq. (2.7):

$$\frac{S_T}{S_{total}} = \frac{g_T}{g} = \frac{\Delta P}{P} = \frac{t_{d,T}}{t_d} < p \ . \tag{2.7}$$

We came to the conclusion that the sizes of the respective Trojan and circuit play a significant role in assessing the attack probability. It is more likely that an attacker will try to insert a relatively small Trojan in a large circuit due to the low detection rate. The cost of injecting Trojans is discussed in Section 2.4.5.

2.4.4   ACTIVATION PROBABILITY

In considering the activation probability of a hardware Trojan we have to analyze two sides. On the one hand, the hardware manufacturer wants to activate the Trojan during a functional test in order to detect and remove it from its circuit. On the other hand, the attacker aims to keep the activation probability as low as possible in order to pass the manufacturer's tests while also leaving an open backdoor for the later activation scenario.

However, the activation probability of a Trojan is mainly based on the circuit's number of primary inputs e as well as the Trojan's inputs e_T. One of the most basic approaches is that the Trojan is waiting for a specific bit pattern at its input vector. As already mentioned in Section 2.4.1, the number of possible input combinations is $E = 2^e$ (cf. Eq. (2.2)). In the example case of an input vector $e = 32$, the manufacturer has to test $E = 2^{32} = 4294967296 \approx 4.3$ billion input combinations. In the case that a test frequency of $f = 10MHz$ is used for the circuit, the test time amounts to $t_{Test} = 1/f = 1/10MHz = 10.10^{-9}s = 10ns$, and thus the total test time of the circuit amounts to $t_{Test,total} = E * t_{Test} = 43s$. The total test time of $43s$ is a reasonable and still manageable effort, but if the input vector is raised to 40, the test time shows a strong increase to $10995s$, which is about 183 min or 3 h test time per circuit. Obviously, a test time of such an extent is not economically feasible, and we, therefore, use test methods that drastically decrease the required test time but do not cover all possible input combinations.

We determine the activation possibility within a functional test with the following Eq. (2.8):

$$P_{act} = \frac{1}{2^e} \ . \tag{2.8}$$

From this we can derive that the larger the number of tested vectors, the larger the possibility to activate and detect an implemented hardware Trojan. Furthermore, the characteristics of known hardware Trojans can be used as test parameters in order to decrease the test time while keeping the detection rate at a constant level.

2.4.5 IMPLEMENTATION COSTS

The implementation costs of a Trojan are based mainly on the injection phase of the production process (cf. Section 2.3.4). For instance, using the design phase for injection is obviously more cost effective than reverse engineering the circuit. By reverse engineering, the physical representation of the circuit is reproduced so that a suitable injection area for the Trojan is found, whereas in the design phase, the designer of the circuit only has to insert the malicious code. This means high material, infrastructural, and personnel costs in the production phase, while in the design phase, only personnel costs are relevant. We determine the attack cost with Eq. (2.9).

$$K_{attack} = K_{material} + K_{infrastructural} + K_{personnel} \, . \qquad (2.9)$$

Furthermore, in the case of reverse engineering, the attacker has to be highly skilled and trained for the reverse engineering procedure as well as for the handling of the respective infrastructure, which makes the personnel costs higher for reverse engineering than for injection in the design phase.

From Section 2.3.4 and Eq. (2.9), we can conclude that the costs rise with decreasing abstraction level due to rising material, infrastructural, and personnel costs.

2.4.6 DETECTION COSTS

The detection costs are mainly determined by the actual injection phase, similar to the implementation costs (cf. Section 2.4.5). However, in the case of attack costs, we are only interested in the phase in which the Trojan is to be injected. In the case of detection costs, we have to consider all phases by analyzing all possible insertion points of the attacker, and thus the costs of the phases are added up. Nevertheless, detection methods before tape-out are more cost-efficient than detection methods after tape-out.

The design of the respective circuit already exists in a machine-understandable specification. In theory, it is possible to compare the design and the final implementation, and thus find abnormalities that reveal the presence of a Trojan. However, this is hardly possible in practice due to the non-reversible characteristics of applied specification languages. For instance, the language does not always specify in detail how the circuit should exactly work. Instead, the respective output is important and more than one way could lead to the same result, so that specification and implementation are not always comparable.

Therefore, detection after tape-out requires skilled staff trained in the area of hardware Trojans as well as the availability of the required infrastructure for testing. Furthermore, we depend heavily on reference circuits to distinguish compromised from authentic hardware.

The detection costs are determined as the sum of all phases according to Eq. (2.10):

$$K_{detection} = \sum_i (K_{material,i} + K_{infrastructural,i} + K_{personnel,i}) . \qquad (2.10)$$

In conclusion, the more injection phases are possible, the higher the estimated detection costs.

CHAPTER 3

Countermeasures

There are many ways of dealing with the risk of hardware Trojans. This chapter discusses mechanisms for *detection*, *localization*, and *prevention* of hardware Trojans. Figure 3.1 shows the different categories.

Detection   Determines whether a hardware system contains an unspecified functionality.

Localization   If a detection mechanism diagnosed the examined system as compromised, a *localization* mechanism determines the topological (logical and/or physical) position of the Trojan.

Prevention   Inhibits the inclusion of Trojans into hardware.

This chapter will address these approaches in detail.

3.1   INTRODUCTION AND CHALLENGES

There is no single method ("silver bullet" cf Chakraborty et al. [20], Zhang and Tehranipoor [91]) against malware in silicon circuits. Every method targets a specific stage of the design flow where the integrity of the circuits could have been corrupted and covers a specific Trojan model (i.e., combinatorial or sequential) that the respective authors assume. While pre-silicon methods focus on validation, verification and backward-traceability of the design and layout (in case the Trojan was inserted during design or layout), post-silicon methods try to validate the final product. Some methods require a so-called golden model, which is a (set of) genuine unmodified reference model(s) for measuring and deriving reference values for testing shipped products. However, process variations make it impossible to derive these values with the needed precision solely from simulations in most cases. Therefore, physical golden models often have to undergo a very resource-intensive and time-consuming procedure of destructive verification using reverse engineering techniques. Changes in the production process might require the procedure to be repeated.

These measured values form a fingerprint of a genuine IC for final product testing. Outliers will be assumed to be modified and might undergo additional testing and analysis. However, changes in these values depend largely on the relationships between process variations, measurement noise, size[1] of the original circuit, and size of the inserted Trojan. As circuit structures shrink with every new fabrication generation, the share of process variations and noise grows.

---

[1]and indirectly also *complexity*

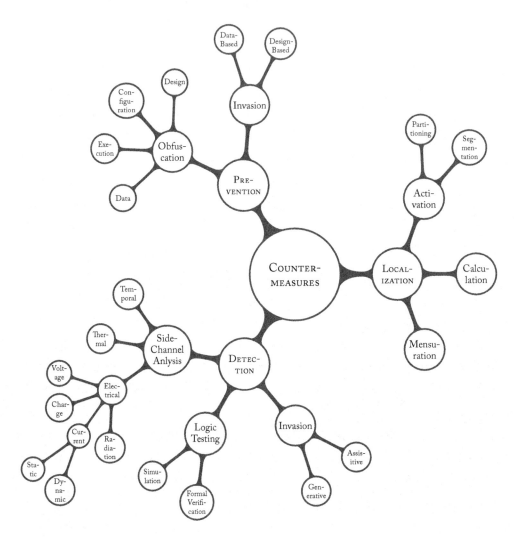

Figure 3.1: Measures against hardware Trojans.

Furthermore, detection sensitivity suffers in multi-million gate designs as a Trojan will introduce relatively small changes (cf. Narasimhan and Bhunia [55]). The latter is addressed by partitioning and segmentation techniques.

To aid detection, verification and localization of Trojans during test time as well as run-time, several methods introduce additional circuitry or other design changes. Non-destructive tests focus on logic testing and side-channel analysis. Side channels are typically physical effects occurring inside or around a circuit that do not play a part in its primary function, and as such, they were ignored for a long time. Side channels include switching (or transient) current transient current (I_{DDT}) caused by gates changing their states, quiescent current, which leaks through gates regardless of their state changes, or (electromagnetic) radiation caused by moving currents.

Regardless of the Trojan model, test time and runtime methods generally assume that an attacker is not aware of these countermeasures. At the end of this chapter we will shed some light on several anti-countermeasure techniques known so far.

The authors want to stress that different research groups use different test sets to validate their approaches. Therefore, the success rates presented below should be handled carefully and are not always comparable. Furthermore, some approaches need further investigations on scalability and practicability, as verifications have been conducted within small simulations.

3.2   DETECTION

One transition in the life cycle of an IC is of major importance: the transmission of the logical representation of the chip (e.g., GDSII file) to the mask manufacturer (*tape-out*, cf. Section 2.3.1 and Figure 2.8). At this point, the design is about to get a concrete, physical form, first as photo mask and then in hardware, and with that, the methods of testing and verification change fundamentally.

During the design and development phase, malicious functionality could be found through *formal verification* or *simulation*. After production, however, the detection is possible exclusively by *logic tests* and *side-channel analysis*.

3.2.1   FORMAL VERIFICATION

Formal equivalence checking is a method for checking the equivalence of two representations of a design (e.g., hardware description and netlist) (cf. Smith and Di [73]). For instance, Zhang and Tehranipoor [91] presented a complementary flow intended to detect suspicious signals with formal verification and conducted a case study on RS232 circuits. It is often implemented as a reverse test, checking the outcome of one of the generation or synthesis chain steps to the previous representation. A test against a model is called *formal model checking*.

3.2.2 SIMULATION

The behavior of a system can be verified with simulation by making assumptions for states and input conditions and then monitoring the resulting states and outputs.

3.2.3 LOGIC TESTING

During logic tests, test patterns are applied to the primary inputs of the chip. The results on the primary outputs are compared to expected results. However, in a typical design the input and state space is huge so that an extraordinarily large number of test patterns is required for full coverage. Scan tests allow setting states more directly, thereby reducing the needed effort significantly.

Moreover, Trojans are designed to conceal their existence and, therefore, to activate only at the occurrence of a very rare event (state, inputs). Hence, the probability that a Trojan is detected using random test patterns is very low (cf. Waksman and Sethumadhavan [82]).

To address this problem, recent publications have proposed approaches for generating test patterns for the detection of Trojans by targeting these rare events usually not found during normal operations (cf. Sreedhar et al. [74]).

Chakraborty et al. [22] presented an approach that determines rare states using a statistical analysis on the netlist of a design. Based on this analysis, test patterns that specifically cause rare states are generated. By repeatedly applying the same test patterns to the primary inputs of a chip, even sequential Trojans that count occurrences of events should be activated. Experimental tests show that the test time can be reduced by 85% compared to random tests. Moreover, the method is also suitable for the detection of smaller sequential Trojans.

In 2010, Narasimhan et al. [56] presented test patterns that are based on the activity of circuit components. First, the netlist of a design is partitioned into smaller, non-overlapping modules. By analyzing the connectivity as well as testing with random test patterns, test patterns that cause high circuit activity will be determined. The activity of other modules is kept low. Then, the authors enhance a modified version of the statistical test pattern generator described above (cf. Chakraborty et al. [22]) is applied that aims for these rare activation patterns. The approach attempts to reach parts of the circuit that would otherwise be difficult to activate or would not activate at all. Experimental tests show that the proposed method—in combination with a side-channel analysis using I_{DDT}—is appropriate for the detection of large, sequential Trojans.

Banga and Hsiao [12] generated test patterns in order to partition a circuit based on the Hamming distance of the state variables. The Hamming distance of state variables between two consecutive states is intended to be maximized to activate as many different parts as possible. On the other hand, the Hamming distances of remaining state variables are minimized so that only one specific part of the circuit is active during the test.

Chakraborty and Bhunia [24] and Chakraborty et al. [21] use obfuscation to make the state space hard to attack. If a Trojan has been injected, a state that is difficult to reach could be transformed into state that is supposedly easy to reach. An attack can, therefore, be detected more easily during a logic test.

3.2.4 SIDE-CHANNEL ANALYSIS

Side-channel analysis examines the physical parameters of a chip not primarily intended for information processing and transmission, such as supply current, temperature, and electromagnetic emanation (cf. Agrawal et al. [4], Banga [9], Banga et al. [11]). Manipulated chips can be detected by comparing them with trusted, Trojan-free reference chips (golden models).

Taxonomy

Figure 3.2 shows a classification of the physical side channels that have been used for analysis so far. These can be divided into electrical, thermal, and temporal side channels.

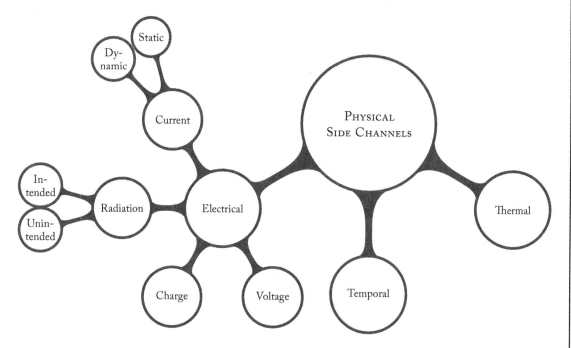

Figure 3.2: Classification of the physical side channels.

Temporal   side channels are generated by the signal delay due to propagation delays of gates. If additional gates are inserted, the performance of the entire IC changes. Temporal side channels are exploited in work proposed by Jin and Makris [37], Koushanfar and Mirhoseini [46], Lamech et al. [49], Li and Lach [50], and Rai and Lach [63].

Thermal   side channels arise from temperature fluctuations due to the operation of the IC. If a part of the circuit is active, this is reflected in an increase in temperature, which is used by Kean et al. [40] to authenticate ICs .

Electrical voltage based side channels exploit the fact that switching gates or transistors have a measurable impact on the supply voltage and current. This type of side channel is sometimes used by a Trojan to leak information. However, it can also be used to detect Trojans as described by Zhang and Tehranipoor [92] in 2011. A network of ring oscillators is utilized as power monitor of certain parts of the IC. A Trojan will likely change power and noise signature of some parts of the circuit. By employing several ring oscillators in different parts of the circuit, Zhang and Tehranipoor [92] are confident that they can distinguish Trojans and process variations.

Electrical static current —also quiescent current or I_{DDQ}—is defined as the current that flows regardless of switching operations. Aarestad et al. [1] use quiescent current for the detection of Trojans. Due to decreasing feature size, in modern designs, variations of leakage surpass static currents that might have been introduced by a Trojan.

Electrical dynamic current —transient current or I_{DDT}—is defined as the current that is caused by switching operations. The transient current is used in several work (cf. Koushanfar and Mirhoseini [46], Rad et al. [60, 61, 62]) to detect Trojans. This analysis is based on the fact that a (partially) active Trojans draws more current than a reference chip without any Trojan as side channel.

Electrical charge as side channel is used to make the small effects of a Trojan visible. Here, I_{DDT} is integrated over the test period, resulting in a continuous increase in charge. At the end of the test period, the difference between the accumulated charge and the charge of a reference chip is investigated. If the difference is above a certain threshold, the presence of a Trojan is assumed. (cf. Wang et al. [83])

Intended radiation serves as a hidden channel for a Trojan to leak data. Jin and Makris [38] employ this to leak a previously obtained Advanced Encryption Standard (AES) key via a covert radio signal.

Unintended radiation in this context is electromagnetic radiation that is used for the detection of a Trojan. The radiation is caused by the action of the Trojan. However, it is completely unintentional and has no benefit for the attack. So far, no application is known that detects a Trojan using unintended radiation, but it shall be mentioned here for the sake of completeness.

General Aspects

Figure 3.3 visualizes the typical flow of Trojan detection. The basis of every side-channel analysis is a functional test. Test patterns are ideally crafted in a way that undermines the efforts of a Trojan to remain hidden, as described in Section 3.2.3 (Automated Test Pattern Generation (ATPG)).

Multiple side channels can also be measured simultaneously (cf. Koushanfar and Mirhoseini [46], Lamech et al. [49]). Supply voltage (cf. Zhang and Tehranipoor [92]), transient cur-

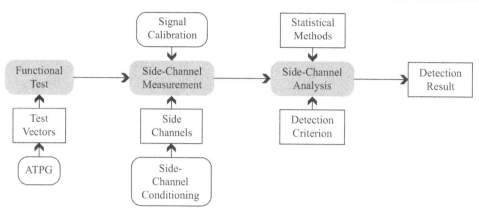

Figure 3.3: Usual flow of a side-channel analysis.

rent I_{DDT} (cf. Koushanfar and Mirhoseini [46], Rad et al. [60, 61, 62]), performance (cf. Jin and Makris [37], Koushanfar and Mirhoseini [46], Lamech et al. [49], Li and Lach [50], Rai and Lach [63]) and switching power (cf. Lamech et al. [49], Wei et al. [85]) have proven to be most suitable.

As Trojans are designed to avoid recognition, we assume that they try to minimize their impact on power consumption, delay and area used. Furthermore, as semiconductor dimension shrink process variations increase (cf. Unsal et al. [80]). It is therefore becoming more and more likely that measurable effects of Trojans are of the same order of magnitude as the impact of process variations and are therefore getting more difficult to distinguish.

Calibration

In order to account for process variations, the measurement process should be preceded by a *calibration* to minimize its effects.

Rad et al. [62] describe a method that is based on current measurement and normalization thereof. The supply current is measured at multiple power ports across the entire chip area. Figure 3.4(a) shows the distribution of the power ports (PP_0 to PP_8). During calibration, each of these points is excited with a current step, and the step response is recorded at each power port. Figure 3.4(b) shows the step responses. It is apparent that the largest absolute value is recorded at the point where the current step is applied (in this case PP_0). Since the resistance grows with distance from the power port, correspondingly smaller absolute values result for the other power ports. This kind of procedure is followed for each power port. The result is a matrix with the measurements (lines) for each power port (columns). Each element is normalized (with the sum of the line elements). By inversion, a transformation matrix is created, which is subsequently used to calibrate the measurements. The supply current is measured while the functional tests are performed.

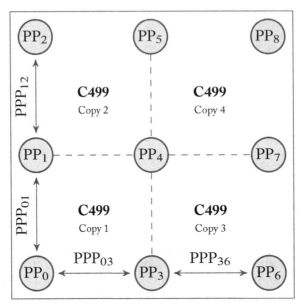

(a) Arrangement of the power ports on the chip area

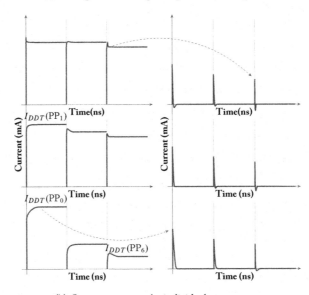

(b) Step responses at the individual power ports

Figure 3.4: Calibration technique as described by Rad et al. [62].

It is evident that a higher number of calibration points results in more accurate measurements. If the grid of the calibration points is continually refined, the matrix for calibration of the measurement results also grows. Such refinement can go as far as to determine a scale factor for each individual gate of a circuit to calibrate the measurement (and thus serve as a calibration point). This method is known as GLC (Gate-Level Characterization).

GLC is suitable for the calibration of different parameters. Wei et al. [85] use the leakage power as the characteristic parameter for the detection of Trojans, whereas Koushanfar and Mirhoseini [46] use the propagation delay of a gate. Nelson et al. [57] characterize gates using both propagation delay and leakage power. As an alternative, Potkonjak et al. [59] propose the characterization of gates using leakage current, switching power und propagation delay.

A GLC involves the following steps: The characteristic parameters (e.g., propagation delay, switching power or leakage current) are measured during a functional test. The test vectors of the functional test determine which gates are involved in the measurement result. The measurements can then be described as a system of linearly independent Eqs. (cf. Wei et al. [85]) (Eq. 3.1).

$$K \cdot s = \tilde{x} + e . \tag{3.1}$$

$K \in R^{m \times n}$ is the coefficient matrix of the characteristic parameter (e.g., performance or timing). It is the "expected" variable with values based on the gate types (e.g., NAND-Gate with two inputs) and the input states (e.g., both inputs at 0). m is the number of measurements, n the number of gates in the chip. The one-dimensional vectors s, $\tilde{x}$, and e represent the scaling factors, the measured values of the parameter (in relation to the entire chip), and the measurement error.

The goal is to determine the scaling factors in order to minimize the effects of the process variations. The measurement error must be kept as low as possible.

The problem is solved using a linear program. Corresponding constraints make it possible to influence the desired results. In this case, the minimization of the measurement error is the constraint (see Eq. 3.2).

$$min \sum_{i=1}^{m} |e_i| . \tag{3.2}$$

The logic gates of a chip can often correlate very strongly, which also makes it more difficult to characterize a gate. To break these correlations, the gates to be measured can be conditioned further. They are made more discriminable by introducing variations. Wei et al. [85] achieve this by heating individual parts of the chip to different temperatures. Since the characteristics of a gate are temperature-dependent, different gates behave differently in terms of their characteristic parameters. For example, the leakage power exponentially grows with temperature.

However, the whole approach requires precise control over temperature and accurate measurements, which are in practice hard to achieve. Academic research in this area is mostly based on simulations.

Golden Model

In order to make a statement about the existence of a Trojan, detection criteria must also be defined. This presumes the existence of a *golden model*. A golden model is a reference model that by definition contains no Trojan.

A golden model can be obtained in two ways:

1. by **destructive testing** and reverse engineering based on optical analysis or

2. by **simulation**, under the assumption of trustworthy developers.

Golden models that are obtained through destructive testing require the presence of chips that are free of Trojans. Some of these chips are initially operated with functional tests to measure the side channels. The measurement results are used to create a "side-channel fingerprint." Afterwards, the chip is stripped layer by layer to optically analyze and reverse engineer the semiconductor structures in order to verify that the chip complies with the original specifications (cf. Agrawal et al. [4]). This method is generally very resource-intensive.

Simulated golden models require that no malicious functionality was introduced during the design phase. By simulating the side-channel analysis, side channel fingerprints are obtained. They are used as a reference for real chips that will be tested. This method is very popular because of its much smaller costs when compared to destructive testing, but is not suitable for all circuits (cf. Rilling et al. [67]). The simulation can consider process variations as introduced by Alkabani and Koushanfar [7], Banga and Hsiao [12, 13, 14], Jin and Makris [37], Potkonjak et al. [59], Rad et al. [62], Wang et al. [83], but, e.g., Li and Lach [50] does not consider process variations.

Analysis

The measurement results are evaluated using statistical methods.

Karhunen-Loéve Analysis   Agrawal et al. [4] use two approaches for statistical analysis. The first approach is a Karhunen-Loéve expansion to obtain the eigenvectors of the process noise of the signals that were measured on Trojan-free reference chips. Subsequently, the mean μ and the standard deviation σ of the spectrum of each eigenvector is determined. To check whether an arbitrary signal is related to a chip with or without a Trojan, the corresponding eigenvector is determined by projection onto the eigenvectors of the process noise. If the eigenvalue spectrum for some eigenvalue is located outside $\mu \pm 4\sigma$, the presence of a Trojan is assumed (Figure 3.5(a)). In the second approach of the statistical analysis, the authors focus on areas with low process noise. Using the Karhunen-Loéve analysis, a clear separation of the eigenvalue spectra of original chips and Trojans can be achieved (Figure 3.5(b)). A specific criterion for Trojan detection, however, is not specified.

Hidden Signals   Jin and Makris [38] presented the analysis of a Trojan's hidden data within a wireless transmission signal. They produced three types of chips: 1. Original chips without malicious circuit; 2. Trojans that alter the amplitude of the transmission signal (Type-I Trojan); and 3. Trojans that alter the phase of the transmission signal (Type-II Trojan).

The power of the transmission signal is used as basis for a side channel. As Figure 3.6(a) illustrates, it is not possible to distinguish between the different types of Trojans. The figure shows the projection of the three types of Trojans onto three out of six dimensions. A dimension is the measured power when transmitting a specific data block. By applying a principal component analysis, however, different types can be grouped (Figure 3.6(b)). By defining a minimum-volume ellipsoid that envelops the data points of the original chip, a criterion for the detection of Trojans is created: all data points that fall outside the ellipsoid indicate the presence of a Trojans.

Regression   Another way of statistical analysis is provided by regression. A regression line based on the measurement results of the side channels is calculated. By defining a confidence interval, a statement can be made about the presence of a Trojan. If a data point resides within the interval, it is very likely to originate from an unmodified chip. Regression is used by Lamech et al. [49] as well as by Aarestad et al. [1]. Lamech et al. [49] analyzed the clock frequency depending on I_{DDT} (see Figure 4.8(a) on p. 76), the range $\pm 3\sigma$ serves as confidence interval around the regression line. Aarestad et al. [1] analyze the values of the quiescent current, which is measured at several supply pads. The currents are then related to adjacent supply pads. If the measured values deviate

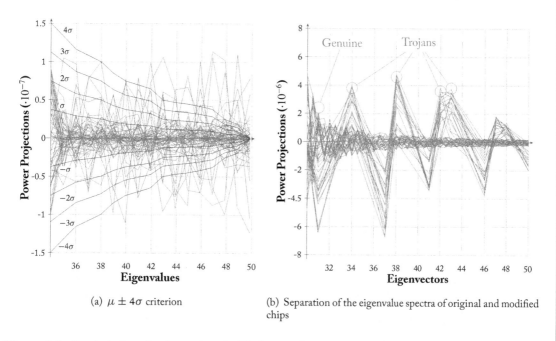

(a) $\mu \pm 4\sigma$ criterion

(b) Separation of the eigenvalue spectra of original and modified chips

Figure 3.5: Statistical evaluation using the Karhunen-Loéve analysis (based on Agrawal et al. [4]).

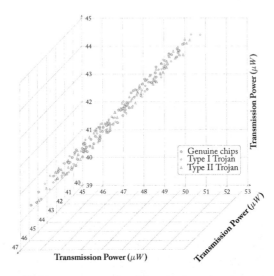

(a) Measurement results of the side-channel analysis

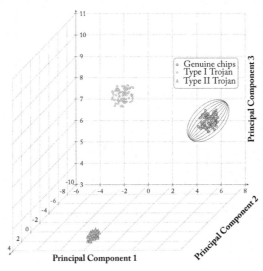

(b) Results of the principal component analysis of the measured power

Figure 3.6: Statistical evaluation using principal component analysis according to Jin and Makris [38].

from the regression line by more than $\pm 3\sigma$, a Trojan is assumed (Figure 3.7). The confidence interval is determined using measurements of 20 reference chips.

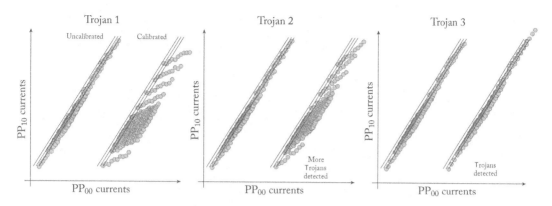

Figure 3.7: Statistical analysis using regression (based on Aarestad et al. [1]).

Nelson et al. [57] use singular value decomposition as detection technique. Based on the scaling factors determined by a GLC, the singular value decomposition is used to create "fingerprints" of the chips. Should the averages of the scaling factors for all gates be higher than the scaling factors for other circuits, the existence of a Trojan is assumed.

Rad et al. [62] perform a statistical analysis on the waveforms of I_{DDT}. Here, the currents of power ports are brought into relation with each other. A scatter plot of measured values is

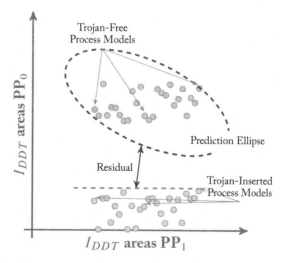

Figure 3.8: Statistical analysis using outlier analysis according to Rad et al. [62].

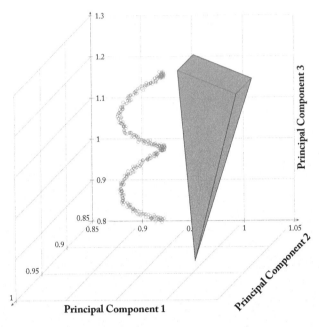

(a) Detection using principal component analysis

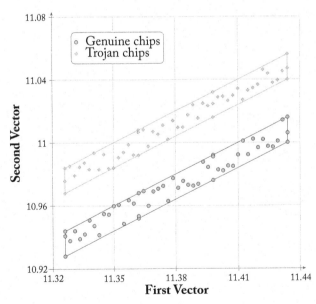

(b) Detection using advanced outlier analysis

Figure 3.9: Statistical analysis using several methods (based on Zhang and Tehranipoor [92]).

created for each chip. A prediction ellipse created from the data points of the first fifteen (out of twenty) Trojan-free simulation models serves as detection criterion. If a data point falls outside of the ellipse it can be assigned to a Trojan (see Figure 3.8). In this context, this method is also called *outlier analysis*.

Outlier analysis is also used by Zhang and Tehranipoor [92]. They define three classes of analyses: 1. simple outlier analysis, 2. principal component analysis, and 3. advanced outlier analysis.

Invasive ring oscillators change their response based on the voltage drop caused by the current consumption of a Trojan. These frequencies act as a signature of the power consumption of the tested chip. Simple outlier analysis checks whether this frequency for a ring oscillator resides within a certain range—if it does not, malicious modification is assumed. After passing this test, the IC has to undergo a principal component analysis. The first three main components of Trojan-free ICs define the convex hull. All data points that fall outside the convex hull are potential Trojans (see Figure 3.9(a)). All data points that lie inside the convex hull are subject to further analysis through advanced outlier analysis. Advanced outlier analysis not only considers the frequency deviation of one component in the ring oscillator network, but also takes into account the relationships between the ring oscillators in the ring oscillator network.

3.2.5   INVASION

The insertion of additional, dedicated circuitry into an existing design is called *invasion*. Although the original design changes, the original functionality remains the same. Invasive approaches to the detection of Trojans usually supplement other detection methods. The invasive methods can be classified according to their relationship to the detection methods they support (Figure 3.10).

Invasive approaches are used to generate test signals that are then analyzed for the influence of Trojans. This is called *generation*. Zhang and Tehranipoor [92] add a network of ring oscillators into an existing design (see p. 80). If a Trojan consumes power, the frequencies of the installed ring oscillators change. By analyzing the frequency changes, the presence of a Trojan can be deduced.

Li and Lach [50] use shadow registers to detect injected Trojans from changes in the system's performance. The delay times of paths are compared to default values. If they deviate considerably, a Trojan could be responsible.

Kean et al. [40] create a side channel from the performance of a system, which is transported to the outside by modulating the frequencies of ring oscillators. The ring oscillators heat up slightly when stimulated so that a side-channel analysis can be performed after temperature measurement.

Lamech et al. [49] install a time-to-digital-converter in that allows high resolution time measurement (see p. 75). The obtained measurements are then subjected to a side-channel analysis to trace possible Trojans that influence the performance.

Invasive methods are also used to influence existing test signals to make it easier to detect Trojans. As the detection is supported, we call this *assistance*.

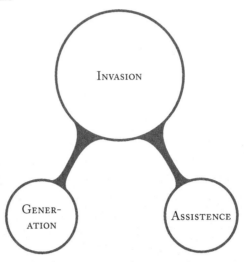

Figure 3.10: Ways of detecting Trojans using invasion.

Salmani et al. [71] use dummy flip-flops to increase the switching probability of circuit parts, which is rather low under normal test conditions (see p. 76). This should increase the activation probabilities of Trojans during functional tests in order to increase the detection rate. The approach can also be combined with a side-channel analysis as additional support.

Banga and Hsiao [14] propose a method to invert the supply voltage within an integrated circuit. The goal is to increase the activation probability of Trojans by reversing the logical functions of gates. The approach can support other methods such as a side-channel analysis. However, this approach has only been verified in simulation and with very small Trojans.

Invasive approaches might also be used to support logic tests. Chakraborty et al. [21] introduce a design method to facilitate the detection of Trojans. Signatures are generated at the primary outputs of a hardware system if specific keys are present on its primary inputs—in other words, if correct test patterns are applied. To create these signatures, the mode of operation is switched to a newly introduced *transparent mode*. In transparent mode, hard-to-control nodes are stimulated and hard-to-observe nodes are monitored. Figure 3.11(a) shows the signature creation for a component of the hardware system: the key inputs stimulate hard-to-control nodes via a control logic. The resulting states of the hard-to-observe nodes are then compacted into a signature that is provided on the signature outputs. The signature propagates from the primary inputs over all existing components to the primary outputs (Figure 3.11(b)). If a signature for a key does not correspond to the expected value, the presence of a Trojan can be assumed.

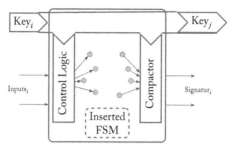

(a) Signature for a component

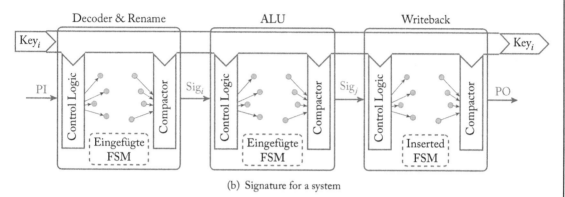

(b) Signature for a system

Figure 3.11: Creation of a signature based on hard-to-observe and hard-to-control nodes according to Chakraborty et al. [21].

3.3   LOCALIZATION

If the inclusion of one or more malicious circuits in a design is detected, the next step is their *localization*. There are different methods of localization depending on the abstraction layer (see Section 2.3.1). Localization is the *regional* detection of a malicious circuit. Figure 3.12 presents the different possibilities for localization.

The currently applied methods of localization are *activation*, *mensuration*, or *calculation*.

3.3.1   ACTIVATION

Localization through *activation* is achieved by activating a subset of gates during the functional test. The goal is to maximize the activity in certain areas of the circuit while minimizing the activity in the remaining areas. This can happen in two ways: by segmentation, which is the fragmentation of the circuit in the state space, or by partitioning, which is the division of the circuit according to its structural composition.

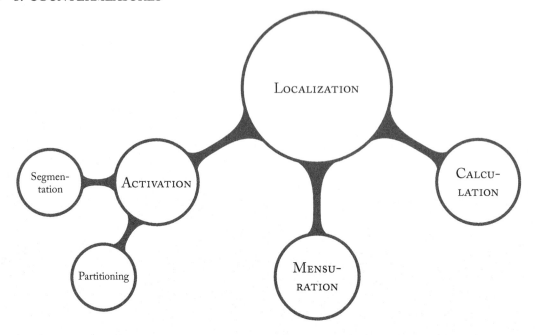

Figure 3.12: Methods for localizing detected Trojans.

Partitioning

Partitioning is the **structural** division of the circuit into several subcircuits.

One approach is based on the Hamming distance of state variables (see p. 34). Banga et al. [11] seeks to generate test patterns that activate a particular part of the circuit (*partition*) while minimizing the activity of other partitions. As a result, the activity in the fan-out cone of the flip-flops contained in the partition is low. If a Trojan is identified in the course of a side-channel analysis, it is located in the partition that was active during the test.

As an alternative, the same authors propose a partition method based on the maximization of the toggle count instead of the Hamming distance (cf. Banga and Hsiao [12]). This is because the Hamming distance does not necessarily permit the drawing of conclusions on the power consumption of a tested circuit. Figure 3.13 shows a sample partitioning of a circuit. The partitions of a circuit (Figure 3.13(a)) result from a fixed *radius*. A radius of 0 means that only one specific gate is included in the partition. A radius of 1 contains a specific gate and the gates upstream and downstream from it that are included in the first level. A radius of 2 extends to the second level, etc.

For example, in Figure 3.13(b) the following gates belong to a radius of 1: G1, G2, G3, G4, FF1, G7, and G6. It is assumed that Trojans are connected to circuit components that fulfill a specific functionality. This functionality is executed by flip-flops and their gates. Therefore, a flip-flop threshold is defined that determines how many flip-flops are present in a partition. In other words: the radius of a partition is extended until the appropriate number of flip-flops is contained in the partition. Afterwards, test patterns are generated to maximize activity within the partitions while the activity in the rest of the circuit is minimized. If a Trojan is subsequently detected through side-channel analysis, it is located in the partition in whose test pattern the Trojan was recognized.

Salmani et al. [70] propose the reorganization of the scan flip-flops in a circuit (see p. 69). During functional tests, a localized activation of circuit parts is achieved by regional grouping of individual scan chains. If a Trojan is detected in the course of a side-channel analysis, it must be sought in the vicinity of the scan chain that was active during its discovery.

Segmentation

Segmentation is the **functional** partitioning of a circuit into subcircuits. This is achieved by variation of input vectors to activate specific gates during a functional test. If a Trojan is detected by applying a specific sequence of test vectors, it is likely to reside in the set of gates—the *segment*—that was addressed by this sequence.

Banga and Hsiao [13] use a technique that keeps a test vector constant for several clock cycles. This is intended to keep the activity of the rest of the circuit low, so that any activity should only originate from inner state changes (see Figures 3.3.1 and 3.3.1). To identify Trojans, the difference in power consumption compared to a non-tempered golden model is determined through side-channel analysis (see Section 3.2.4). A deviation of more than 5% (to account for process variations) might indicate additional circuitry in the vicinity of the logic gates that were stimulated by the test vector. Figure 3.3.1 shows the difference in power of a test vector V_1 at time t. We can see that it is situated in the range around 0%. The next clock cycle, at time $t + 1$, yields

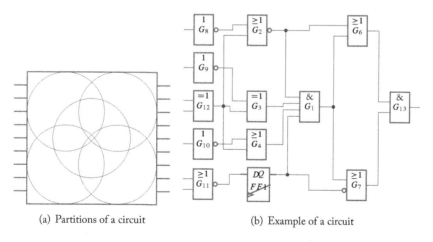

(a) Partitions of a circuit (b) Example of a circuit

Figure 3.13: Partitioning according to Banga and Hsiao [12].

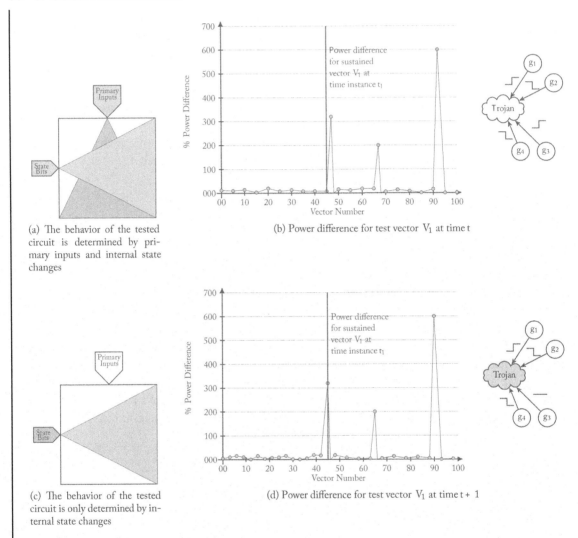

(a) The behavior of the tested circuit is determined by primary inputs and internal state changes

(b) Power difference for test vector V_1 at time t

(c) The behavior of the tested circuit is only determined by internal state changes

(d) Power difference for test vector V_1 at time t + 1

Figure 3.14: Localization through segmentation according to Banga and Hsiao [13].

a power difference that is three times as high as in the unmodified reference model while using the same test vector V_1 (Figure 3.3.1).

Wei et al. [85] follow an approach that finds a subset of gates (a segment) by their controllability by primary inputs. The goal is to produce segments whose gates will have good scaling factors in a subsequent GLC. First, some primary inputs are varied, while the rest of the inputs is held constant. For the resulting segments (the gates that are controlled by primary inputs), a

GLC is performed. The accuracy of the GLC is determined in this step. A regression model is created based on characteristics of the segments as well as the accuracy of the GLC, in order to predict the accuracy of the values of the GLC for other, unknown segments. Trojans are then detected through a side-channel analysis using GLC. If the presence of a Trojan is detected, the segment in which this information was found gives information about its logical position. GLC produces appropriate results in simulations which are in practice hard to achieve, as it requires precise control over temperature and accurate measurements.

Du et al. [31] call for segmentation of a circuit under test into multiple functionally independent blocks.

3.3.2 MENSURATION

Parts of a circuit that have been tampered with can also be localized using the measuring setup that is used for detection. Various methods can be used to capture the side channels that are subsequently evaluated by side-channel analysis.

Rad et al. [62] capture I_{DDT} across multiple power ports scattered across the entire chip surface (see Figure 3.4(a)). The measured current might give clues about the presence of a Trojan. If a significant deviation from I_{DDT} is observed near a power port, a Trojan is suspected in its proximity.

Zhang and Tehranipoor [92] use a network of ring oscillators that are distributed over the entire chip area to determine measurement variables. Figure 3.15 shows the arrangement of the ring oscillators as well as the locations of several implanted Trojans. If Trojans are built into the chip, they alter the frequency of neighboring ring oscillators. This fact can be used to determine the spatial position of a Trojan.

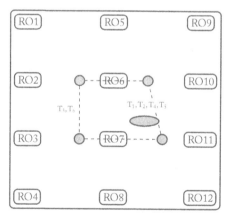

Figure 3.15: Arrangement of ring oscillators and Trojans on the chip surface based on Zhang and Tehranipoor [92].

3.3.3 CALCULATION

A Trojan can also be located with mathematical methods.

GLC (see Section 3.2.4) characterizes circuits at gate level, which means that scaling factors are determined for each individual gate of a circuit in order to calibrate for process variations. If scaling factors differ strongly from their expected values, the presence of a Trojan can be assumed. Because a Trojan influences the scaling factors of the gates to which it is connected, this can be a good clue for its localization (cf. Koushanfar and Mirhoseini [46]).

3.4 PREVENTION

In contrast to detection and localization, *prevention* aims to never even permit Trojans and their actions. Prevention is possible in two ways: by obfuscation and by invasion.

3.4.1 OBFUSCATION

Obfuscation is a method for distorting parts of a hardware system in a way that makes it very difficult, if not impossible, to modify a system or study its functions. Obfuscation can occur at various levels. Figure 3.16 illustrates how they relate to each other.

Design   The *design* of a hardware system is obfuscated at design level to make it impossible (or infeasible) for an attacker to identify the function of a circuit.

Obfuscation by configuration   means that parts of a hardware system are reconfigurable and their final form is determined just before its deployment.

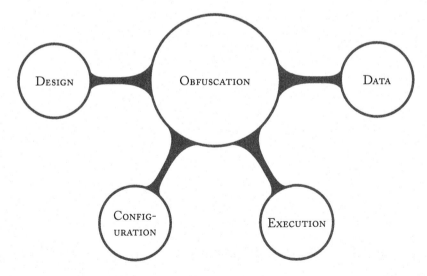

Figure 3.16: Methods of obfuscation.

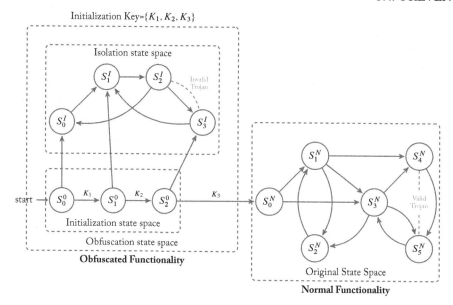

Figure 3.17: Obfuscation of the design according to Chakraborty and Bhunia [24].

Obfuscation by execution has the executed functionality present in several versions so that various paths of execution can be used.

Data can be obfuscated by simple encryption or reordering.

Design

The obfuscation of the design of a hardware system aims to make reverse engineering of the function as hard as possible.

In order to obfuscate the design at gate level, Chakraborty and Bhunia [23] propose an approach that changes the original functionality of the design by modifying the netlist. An additional state machine is inserted that has two execution modes: an obfuscated and a non-obfuscated mode. At the beginning of operations, the state machine is in the obfuscated mode and remains there until a particular pattern is applied to the primary inputs. While in obfuscated mode, invalid data is returned on the primary outputs. When the change from obfuscated to non-obfuscated mode occurs, a transition to a state of the original state machine takes place. This method can prevent the insertion of Trojans because it makes reverse engineering, and therefore the insertion of malicious circuits by an attacker, significantly more difficult.

Chakraborty et al. [21] introduce a method that inserts additional inputs and outputs, and an additional state machine. Authentication keys are generated by the additional circuit components, which will propagate through the entire hardware system. This is done in a special execution mode, the *transparent mode* (see also p. 46), which is activated at test time. The authors note that it is more difficult for an attacker to reverse engineer the original functionality because of the added obfuscation through the additional circuit components.

Chakraborty and Bhunia [24] presented an approach for obfuscation that splits an existing design into two state spaces. One state space implements the original functionality, and the other implements the obfuscated functionality. The starting point of all operations is the obfuscated state space. The transition from obfuscated to normal state space can only be triggered by a very rare condition. Therefore, an attacker who reverse engineers a design cannot find a suitable place to insert the malicious circuit with certainty. Either a Trojan is added to the obfuscated state space—which renders the Trojan harmless—or it is linked to a supposedly difficult to reach state, which in turn increases its visibility in functional tests. Figure 3.17 illustrates the principle. The starting point is a state in the obfuscated space, the initialization state space. To reach the normal state space, a special sequence of states $S_0^O \rightarrow S_1^O \rightarrow S_2^O$ must be traversed. This is only possible if the values K_1, K_2, K_3 are provided at the primary inputs. This sequence of values is called the initialization key. If an invalid key is provided during the initialization phase, a transition into a state is enforced that is part of an isolation state space, which cannot be left. In this way, potential Trojans are rendered harmless. Furthermore, Banga and Hsiao [16] presented a method to not only ease detection of hardware Trojans but to partially obfuscate a design against Trojan implementations. The main goal of this approach is to initially increase the number of reachable states and then to partition the flip-flops into different groups to enhance the state-space variation. In their approach, the state-space variation operate as an obfuscation technique.

Configuration

Obfuscation can also be achieved by *configuration*. One part of the circuit is realized as reconfigurable logic, i.e., as Field-Programmable Gate Array (FPGA). Essential functions of the hardware system are implemented into this reconfigurable part of the chip. The functionality is added to the reconfigurable logic after the chip is provided by the manufacturer and inserted into the application. As shown in Figure 2.11 (p. 20), this will likely happen during the *deployment* phase, while *assembling* the system.

Abramovici and Bradley [2] implement such an approach, as shown in Figure 3.18. The figure shows a system that is intended to avoid attacks altogether or prevent successful attacks from executing. Signals will be tapped by signal processor networks (SPN) which are monitored by security monitors (SM). A security and coordination processor (SECOPRO) configures SPN (which signals should be checked), as well as SM (which tests are done). If the SECOPRO detects unauthorized behavior, it can influence the signals of the hardware system by using signal control. All configurations are stored securely in an encrypted flash memory that makes the reverse engineering of the logic by an attacker virtually impossible. The actual configuration is only taken during operation. The manufacturer does not know its shape and therefore cannot make any changes.

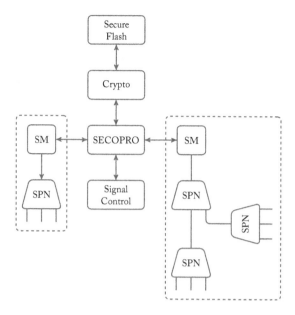

Figure 3.18: Prevention by obfuscation using reconfigurable logic according to Abramovici and Bradley [2].

Execution

Another method of obfuscation uses the *execution* of software on non-trustworthy hardware.

McIntyre et al. [54] use a multi-core system on which different cores are running instances of functionally equivalent software (different algorithms or different compilations of the same algorithm). The approach is based on the assumption that a Trojan is activated on occurrence of a rare event. It is unlikely that two different versions of functionally equivalent software satisfy the same rare condition and thereby activate the same Trojan. Figure 3.19 illustrates the concept. Initially, two different versions A and B are executed on two cores of the hardware system (Figures 3.19(a) and 3.19(b)). If the results V_A and V_B of both executions are the same ($V_A = V_B$), it can be assumed with great certainty that no Trojan has been triggered. If the two results differ ($V_A \neq V_B$), it is assumed that a Trojan has been triggered on one core. Another variant of the task, C, is started (Figure 3.19(c)). If the result of this execution V_C is the same as one of the other results, this means that the Trojan was activated in the core where the execution delivers a different result. If all three results are different ($V_A \neq V_B \neq V_C$), another variant D is started (Figure 3.19(d)) and so on. In order to avoid execution of tasks on compromised cores, the level of trust is reduced for each core on which a Trojan is detected. This allows a scheduler to avoid allocating a compromised core. Such a scheduler is presented by the same authors in McIntyre et al. [53].

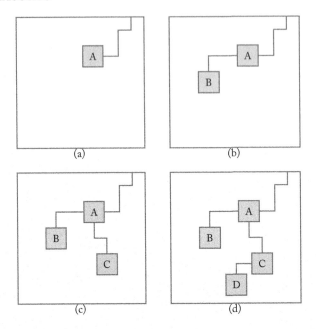

Figure 3.19: Prevention by obfuscation using different variants of functionally equivalent software according to McIntyre et al. [53].

Data

Data can also be obfuscated during the operation of a hardware system to prevent a Trojan's payload. The basic idea is that the trigger condition for a Trojan cannot occur.

Waksman and Sethumadhavan [82] define two types of triggers that can activate a Trojan: *single-shot cheat codes*, and *sequence cheat codes*. In addition, two types of functional units of a hardware system are defined: computational units and non-computational units. Data is obfuscated at inputs to untrusted functional units and de-obfuscated at their outputs (Figure 3.20(a)). Single-shot cheat codes can be obfuscated by simple encryption (such as bitwise XOR or the addition of a random value, see Figure 3.20(a)). However, this is only possible for non-computational functional units. For computational units, homomorphic functions are used. A function f is homomorphic with respect to another function g if (Eq. 3.3):

$$f(x)g(y) = g(f(x,y)) . \tag{3.3}$$

A simple example is the function in Eq. 3.4.

$$x^2 y^2 = (xy)^2 . \tag{3.4}$$

Suppose a functional unit implements the squaring function (see Equation 3.4). To obfuscate the original value x, it is multiplied by a random value y. The functional unit calculates

$(xy)^2$. For de-obfuscation, the result of the functional unit must be divided by the square of the random value y^2, which gives the original result of the functional unit, x^2. In this way, a valid trigger condition should be prevented from occurring for a Trojan within a functional unit. To obfuscate sequences of values, data streams are rearranged in a way that prevents the occurrence of a trigger condition caused by the sequence (Figure 3.20(b)). In cases where it is not possible to rearrange the data stream, dummy values are inserted to break the sequence.

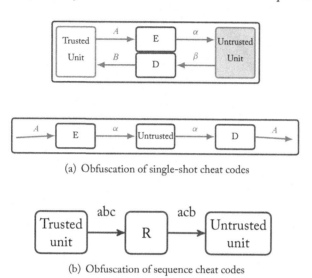

(a) Obfuscation of single-shot cheat codes

(b) Obfuscation of sequence cheat codes

Figure 3.20: Prevention by obfuscation using simple encryption and reordering of data according to Waksman and Sethumadhavan [82].

3.4.2 INVASION

To prevent Trojans, additional functionality can be inserted into a hardware design. This is called *invasion*.

As Figure 3.21 illustrates, invasion can be based on the design of a hardware system or the data to be processed.

If an invasive approach is *design-based*, a hardware design is altered so that Trojans can be defended during operation.

If the data to be processed is monitored during operation, the invasive approach is *data-based*.

A data-based invasive approach can be implemented in two ways: If the added circuitry monitors the authenticity of data, we speak of *guards*. If, on the other hand, the added circuitry modifies data of an application to render them useless for a trigger condition, we speak of *transformation*.

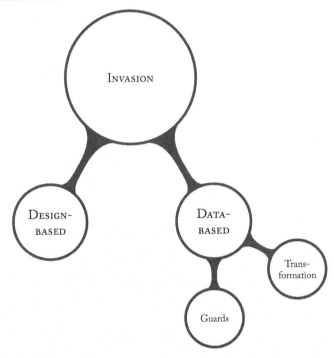

Figure 3.21: Techniques to prevent Trojans by invasion.

Design

A design-based invasive approach to prevent Trojans modifies the original design.

Huffmire et al. [35] propose the introduction of a separate security layer for 3D hardware systems. 3D hardware systems are hardware systems that consist of several stacked and interconnected layers. The security layer is used to perform security tasks such as cryptography. The possibility of defending against hardware Trojans is mentioned briefly but details are left to future research.

Hicks et al. [32] replace suspicious components of a circuit by software emulation. Suspicious components are determined during the functional test at design time. A functional unit counts as suspicious if it is not activated during the entire testing process and could therefore act as a trigger for a Trojan. This method is called Unused Circuit Identification (UCI). If the input and the output of a functional unit have the same value during the entire testing process, the component counts as inactive and can be replaced by a short circuit. To still be able to maintain the functionality of the hardware system, suspicious units are replaced by detection hardware and the original function is emulated by software. Figure 3.22 illustrates the principle.

Sturton et al. [75] proved that circuits exist that are classified as non-suspicious by UCI but can still be used as Trojans (cf. p. 77).

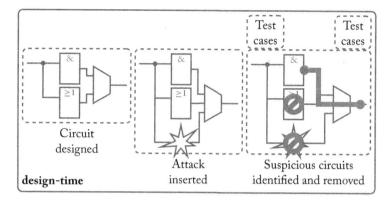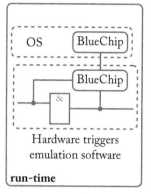

Figure 3.22: Principle of preventing Trojans by software emulation according to Hicks et al. [32].

Guards

A data-based invasive approach can be implemented as a *guard*. The job of a guard is to check and verify processed data for authenticity. If it recognizes that data is invalid or that data is being accessed without permission, it can initiate defensive measures.

Kim et al. [42] and Kim and Villasenor [43] propose Trojan-resistant bus architecture with functionality largely based on data guards. The proposed architecture offers protection against malicious bus masters and malicious bus slaves. Malicious bus masters access memory without authorization. If this is detected, the master is denied access to the bus by the secure address decoder. Malicious masters can also block the bus by locking it by issuing a *lock* signal so that other masters can no longer access the bus. This is prevented by a maximum timespan for which a

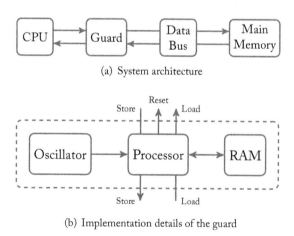

(a) System architecture

(b) Implementation details of the guard

Figure 3.23: Data guard to block malicious access to the memory bus according to Bloom et al. [19].

master can request exclusive bus access. Once this timespan is over, the secure bus arbiter revokes the access of the bus master to the bus. Malicious bus slaves can block the bus by continuously sending a *wait* signal. This problem is addressed in the same manner as a continuous *lock* signal: if a bus slave claims the bus for too long, its access is revoked by a secure bus matrix. If a Trojan is detected, an interrupt signal is sent to initiate further defensive measures.

Bloom et al. [19] introduce a data guard to prevent Denial-of-Service (DoS)-attacks. The data guard has a simple design so that its authenticity can be verified with simple measures. In addition, it is located off-chip. The proposed approach should protect a computer system from DoS-attacks. To counter DoS-attacks, the guard checks if the higher-level operating system is still running. For this purpose, the guard monitors all accesses to the memory (Figure 3.23(a)). The operating system sends a *liveness check* to the guard every 1 μs. The liveness check is implemented as pseudorandom non-cached memory access. The guard detects the liveness check and sets an internal watchdog timer to a pseudorandom value. If the watchdog times out, it assumes that the operating system is no longer running—a DoS-attack is detected. The CPU is reset to allow further operation. Figure 3.23(b) shows implementation details of the guard. An oscillator is used as internal timer, RAM is used to store pseudorandom values. A *reset* signal is used to reset the

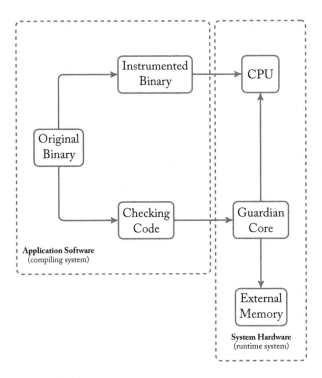

Figure 3.24: Guardian core according to Das et al. [29], to block malicious access to the memory bus.

CPU or to inform a higher-level instance of attack. A processor takes control and monitors the memory bus (*load* and *store* signals).

Waksman and Sethumadhavan [81] present a predictor/monitor/reactor-model, which checks the functional units of a hardware system for authenticity (see p. 70). The monitor takes on the role of guard by comparing predicted values with actual results. Figure 4.2(b) shows implementation details of the monitor. If the values do not match, a Trojan attack is assumed. An alarm is issued to initiate countermeasures.

Das et al. [29] base their work on the assumption that data always has to pass through the main memory before it can leak. Thus, if malicious access to the memory can be prevented, the leakage of data can be prevented. This is achieved by replication of memory operations which are performed by a software application. The source code of the application is altered to create two simultaneous data streams: the original one and a parallel one, for which the addresses are generated using a secret key (see the left part of Figure 3.24). Both data streams are compared to each other, making it possible to detect if the original data stream is manipulated by a Trojan. The data streams are compared by an external guard, which is placed between the CPU and the main memory (see the right part of Figure 3.24). The approach is a combined hardware-/software solution. The software is manipulated by the end-user to create a second data stream with its own keys. The guard core is also programmable, so that the end-user can determine its implementation herself.

Transformation

Another possibility for a data-based invasive approach is to transform the processed data in a way that renders them unusable for a Trojan. The goal is to prevent the trigger from being activated.

Waksman and Sethumadhavan [82] use two types of transformation: *encryption* and *permutation* (cf. pp. 79 and 56). To implement the encryption, additional hardware modules need to be included in the original design. Since the mechanisms can be kept very simple, simple blocks can be inserted at the inputs of computational units for encryption. For decryption, they can be placed at their outputs. In order to permute data within a data stream, the memory control is altered in a simple manner.

In Bloom et al. [18] present an invasive approach which uses dual encryption. Figure 3.25(a) shows the architecture of the approach. An external and an internal guard are implemented, both located between the CPU and the main memory (see Figure 3.25(a)) to defend against attacks to leak data from the main memory. The guards each use a different key sk_1 and sk_2 (see Figure 3.25(b)). The transformation is performed within the guards. If data w should be written to the main memory, it is encrypted by the internal guard ($w_1 = E(sk_1, w)$). The external guard encrypts the output of the internal guard ($w_2 = E(sk_2, w_1)$). The dually encrypted data is then passed on to the main memory. Read access takes place in the opposite order: first data r is decrypted by the external guard ($r_1 = D(sk_2, r)$) and then by the internal guard ($r_2 = D(sk_2, r)$). The memory itself contains only encrypted data. The defense against attacks that leak data is

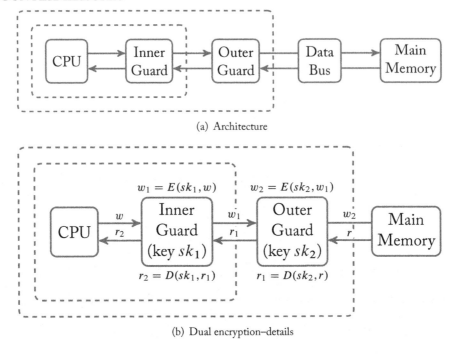

(a) Architecture

(b) Dual encryption–details

Figure 3.25: Prevention by transformation using dual encryption according to Bloom et al. [18].

achieved as follows: if the CPU or the internal guard is compromised, the attack can be defeated by the external guard. Since the outer guard can be made reconfigurable, it is very difficult to compromise.

3.5 CIRCUMVENTING TROJAN COUNTERMEASURES

A large number of the countermeasures proposed above assume that the attacker does not know about them or how they work. However, researchers have found ways around some of these protection schemes. One of them is the careful modification of the layout, so that the physical property used for Trojan detection stays within its margin of confidence. Another method is to mimic its properties without the actual measurement being performed.

The Embedded Systems Competition (ESC) held during the yearly Cyber-Security Awareness Week (CSAW) at the Polytechnic Institute of New York University has picked up this topic several times in the past and named it "Capture the Chip" after the famous series of Capture the Flag contests in computer security. In some years the competing teams had to simply develop a protection scheme, in other years they were given a protected design and had to circumvent it, and one time they had to harden their own chip and attack the hardened chips of the other teams. These types of contests typically give the contestants FPGA boards for development and testing.

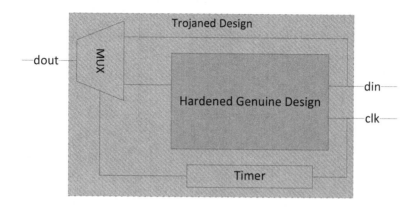

Figure 3.26: Trojan insertion without modification of the genuine design according to Yin et al. [89].

Rilling et al. [67] demonstrated the two ways mentioned above at ESC in 2010. From the two designs given to the teams, Rilling et al. [67] concentrated on the second, called *Beta*. The main security measure built into this design was an adder circuit with several embedded ring oscillators (RO). The idea of the designer was that any design change would alter the length of some of that paths and therefore change the frequencies. The design offered a function that took a challenge value and showed the response on a 7-segment display. However, to account for process variations, the rules allowed a variation of these values by 6.6%.

In its first attempt, the team employed a *design lockdown* technique. From the original design they extracted design placement and routing (P&R) constrains that were subsequently given to the synthesis tool to produce very similar designs of the modified designs. This allowed the team to insert some very small Trojans into the design without disturbing the ring oscillator too much. However, this technique did not allow any bigger changes to be made.

In their second approach, the team created a black-box model of the ring oscillator: it takes a 16-bit input challenge and outputs a 16-bit response. The team realized that some input bits did not play a vital role and that some output pins were de-facto random. They then harvested all remaining 15,360 input combinations using an automated testing environment and found a clever way to compress all the data into 6 kByte memory. Finally, they were able to make any larger modification they wanted to the layout.

After ESC, Rajendran et al. [65] developed a defense strategy against such hardcoding attacks. They realized that the RO also varies with the temperature and the supply voltage (Vdd)—something the design of Rilling et al. [67] did not account for.

Another notable example of the CSAW ESC is from 2009. That year, the teams had to attack designs hardened by other teams while defending (and hardening) their own design. Yin et al. [89] demonstrated a very easy way of bypassing hardening techniques: they built their very lightweight Trojan around the hardened design. In this case, the Trojan simply leaked information by passing the input (plain text) directly to the output pin (usually the cipher text).

CHAPTER 4

Historical Overview

This chapter (an extended version of [93]) provides an overview of the historical development of hardware Trojans and state-of-the art work that facilitates detection and countermeasures in this research area.

4.1 HARDWARE TROJANS: THE BEGINNINGS (2005-2008)

In 2005, the U.S. Department of Defense Defense Science Board, Department of Defense, U.S. [30] released a report on the security of supply of high-performance integrated circuits. In this report, the concept of a vertical business model was investigated for compliance with the demand for secure and authentic hardware. A central statement of the report is that the manufacturing of microchips was relocated to low-wage countries for financial reasons. Therefore, the risk of additional functions being added by chip manufacturers during the production process became realistic. Trustworthiness was described as follows:

> *Trustworthiness* includes confidence that classified or mission critical information contained in chip designs is not compromised, *reliability* is not degraded or unintended design elements inserted in chips as a result of design or fabrication in conditions open to adversary agents. Trust cannot be added to integrated circuits after fabrication; electrical testing and *reverse engineering* cannot be relied upon to detect undesired alterations in military integrated circuits." Defense Science Board, Department of Defense, U.S. [30, p. 3]

As the production processes were partially transferred to potential enemies, the U.S. Department of Defense did not believe that the supply of necessary semiconductors could be ensured in the case of war. For this reason, the research project TRUST in Integrated Circuits (TIC) was launched by the Defense Advanced Research Projects Agency (DARPA) in 2007 (cf. DARPA [28]. TIC is intended to develop technologies that can provide trust for circuits in the absence of a trusted foundry. It only considers technical efforts that address the fabrication of Application-Specific Integrated Circuit (ASIC)s by non-trusted foundries and software implementations of configurable hardware, such as FPGAs.

In the same year, Agrawal et al. [4] published their work on a method for detecting secretly added functionality through side-channel analysis. We consider this work to be the starting point for numerous publications on this topic.

Smith and Di [73] proposed structural verification to detect malicious hardware.

However, it was Adee [3] with her article who triggered a veritable flood of publications. 2008 can be clearly identified as the year in which this topic gained academic interest. The Australian Department of Defence (cf. Anderson et al. [8]) picked up the topic and published a report about the battle against hardware Trojans, evaluating its effectiveness.

The focus at this time was clearly on side-channel analysis (cf. Banga [9], Banga et al. [11], Banga and Hsiao [12], Jin and Makris [37], Li and Lach [50], Rad et al. [60], Tehranipoor and Lee [76], Wang et al. [83]), but other methods such as logic tests (cf. Chakraborty et al. [21]) were proposed as well. In order to improve the detection rate, some approaches were proposed to increase the activation rate of hardware Trojans (cf. Jha and Jha [36], Rad et al. [62]).

King et al. [45] were the first to publish a comprehensive combined hardware/software attack. In this attack, a hardware Trojan serves as the foundation for an extensive attack by allowing an attacker to sign on to the operating system with root privileges supported by a hardware backdoor.

Huffmire et al. [35] proposed a model of a security layer that is applied to 3D hardware systems. This layer can optionally be inserted into security-relevant applications.

The main purpose of the Embedded Systems Challenge is to find appropriate implementations of hardware Trojans and is held on an annual basis by the University of New York. In 2008 and 2010, the major goal of the competition, was to insert *hidden* malicious circuits into the original layout. Furthermore, the amount of secretly extracted information was considered in the final ranking. The work submitted to the competition is summarized by Chen et al. [27] and Baumgarten et al. [17].

In 2008, the international *Workshop on Hardware Security and Trust* was held for the first time with an intense focus on hardware Trojans (cf. HOST [33]).

Wang et al. [84] and Wolff et al. [87] provide first taxonomies and introductions in terms of hardware Trojans.

4.2 HARDWARE TROJANS: A FLOOD OF RESEARCH (2009–2010)

In 2009, a lot of time and effort was invested in further research on methods using side-channel analysis. Side-channel analysis can only be applied reasonably if Trojans are at least partially activated. Other research was directed towards increasing the chance of Trojan activation and, thus, increasing the chance of detection. This can be done by using *toggle minimization* to reduce the overall activity of a circuit, so that we are able to measure the (partial) activity of a Trojan, should one be present (cf. Banga and Hsiao [13]). *Inverting* the *supply voltage* of the logic gates in a circuit causes the logic states of the gates to be inverted as well. This measure causes an inversion of detectability—a Trojan that was hard to spot before can now be detected easily (cf. Banga and Hsiao [14]).

The creation of favorable testing patterns should increase the detection rate for logic tests. Chakraborty et al. [22] present an approach for initiating rare logic states multiple times in order to help trigger potential Trojans. Rare states are identified by a statistical method and chosen on the premise that a Trojan's trigger condition is not activated very often.

Salmani et al. [69] increase the chance of state changes ("toggles") by inserting dummy flip-flops into the original design. Dummy flip-flops are realized as scan flip-flops to preserve the original functionality. This method is widely used in the industry to increase test controllability and coverage.

Technically, side-channel analysis should detect deviations of expected behavior caused by hardware Trojans. We assume that the Trojan's impact is relatively small compared to the overall circuit activity. This is also a problem for detection, because the effect of process variations will be of almost the same order of magnitude. The approach of GLC tries to characterize each gate of an IC. Here, the values of performance, switching power and leakage current are used for characterization. Scaling factors are calculated to account for process variations that cannot be avoided in the manufacturing process. During a functional test, scaling factors are measured with the help of side-channel analysis. If the testing results of an IC differ too much from the calculated characteristics, a Trojan may have been implemented (cf. Nelson et al. [57], Potkonjak et al. [59]).

Specific types of Trojans that have been inserted into complex hardware can also be detected with the help of the operating system. Bloom et al. [19] propose an approach where a simple hardware guard monitors access from the CPU to the memory data bus and performs liveness checks. A watchdog timer is started each time the monitor observes a certain pseudorandom memory access procedure that is initiated by the operating system. If the watchdog times out, a DoS attack is detected. The operating system also periodically checks whether memory protection is activated to prevent privilege escalation attacks.

Kim et al. [42] propose a Trojan-resistant bus architecture for Systems-on-Chip (SoCs). The architecture is able to detect unauthorized bus access. In order to prevent DoS attacks, permanent bus allocation to one bus node is blocked by limiting maximum bus allocation time.

A novel and interesting class of Trojans is introduced by Lin et al. [51]. They present a new technology called *Malicious Off-Chip Leakage Enabled by Side Channels (MOLES)*, which allows the extraction of sensitive data with the help of spread-spectrum technology. Because the signal of the extracted information completely disappears in noise, it is almost impossible to detect the hidden data transfer.

Lin et al. [52] describe how data can be transmitted by modulating the power supply signal using spread-spectrum techniques. The implementation makes use of high capacitances that draw current while charging. Depending on whether a zero or one is to be transmitted, a capacitor is charged or not. The charging current—encoded via spread-spectrum technique—can be analyzed by performing a side-channel analysis on the power supply.

Another approach to detect Trojans in multi-core systems is proposed by McIntyre et al. [54] (cf. Section 3.4.1). In this approach, software is varied while keeping functional equivalence during the execution. This can be accomplished by using different compilations or alternative algorithms. The variants of the software are executed on multiple cores. If one variant of the software matches the trigger condition of an injected Trojan—thus activating it—the results of two calculations will probably differ. This way, a Trojan can be detected and isolated at runtime.

In 2009, there were also a number of international conferences and workshops dedicated to the topic of hardware Trojans (cf. HOST [34], Reconfigurable Computing for Security and Cryptography [66], Workshop on Cryptographic Hardware and Embedded Systems 2009 [88]).

2010 marks a turning point in the detection of Trojans, moving away from detection after production (*post-silicon*) to detection ahead of production (*pre-silicon*).

Banga and Hsiao [15] present an approach that first determines signals that are easy to activate during a functional test. These signals are then ignored when testing for the presence of Trojans that are hard to identify. Using the remaining signals, a formal verification process is triggered. Any detected Trojans are subsequently isolated.

Using an external guardian core, Das et al. [29] propose an approach to prevent data leakage via the data bus caused by hardware Trojans. The watchdog monitors the access behavior to the main memory by comparing each memory access with an emulated version of it. If they match, the memory access is approved by the guard, otherwise it is discarded. The emulation of the memory accesses is done in the software applications that are executed on the system.

The *BlueChip* approach introduced by Hicks et al. [32] also relies on additional hardware modules. It is designed to render hardware Trojans injected at design time harmless at runtime. Trojan isolation is achieved by replacing suspicious hardware with software emulation. Suspicious circuits are identified with UCI, a method that monitors the activity of a circuit during the functional test. If a part of a circuit remains unused during the entire testing period, it is considered to be assigned to a Trojan circuit (which should not be detected during functional tests and would, therefore, remain silent).

Du et al. [31] propose another approach based on side-channel analysis to detect hardware Trojans. The power consumption of a particular region of an IC is compared to the power consumption of the same region of another IC. If the power consumptions differ greatly, the reason could be a Trojan. This technique is called *self referencing*.

Jin and Makris [38] present an attack with which an AES key can be leaked unnoticed by manipulating the transmission signal of a wireless link within its tolerance boundaries. This work is also the first approach in the analog domain.

A comprehensive taxonomy that also considers the different hardware abstraction layers is proposed by Rajendran et al. [64] and Karri et al. [39].

To recognize Trojans at runtime, Keren et al. [41] use error detection mechanisms by applying a 1-to-many code.

Narasimhan et al. [56] partition a layout where the different partitions are stimulated through appropriate test patterns. I_{DDT} and maximum frequency (f_{max}) are determined via side-channel analysis. Because they assume I_{DDT} and f_{max} as linearly dependent and f_{max} as unalterable, a Trojan can be detected by observing an increase of I_{DDT}. However, the production variations do not always allow such general assumptions.

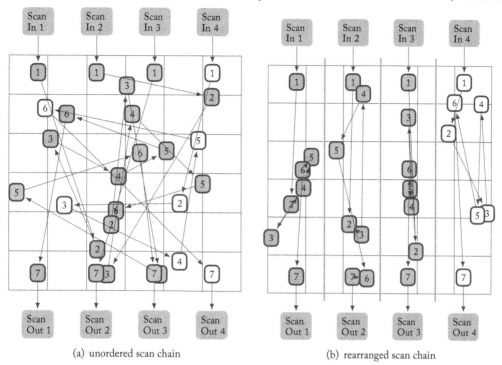

(a) unordered scan chain   (b) rearranged scan chain

Figure 4.1: Comparison of the scan chain layouts (based on Salmani et al. [70]).

To determine the smallest detectable Trojan, Rad et al. [61] examine the sensitivity of a transient analysis of power supply signals. The smallest detectable Trojan consists of a single logic gate under laboratory conditions if the Trojan responds to a test pattern. In their test sample, if the measurement is characterized by a Signal-to-Noise-Ratio (SNR) of 10 dB, the size of the smallest recognizable Trojan increases to seven gates.

Another approach to side-channel analysis is given by Koushanfar et al. [47]. A GLC is performed in several modes: performance, leakage power, and switching power. A voter evaluates the results of the particular modes and provides an assertion about the existence of a Trojan.

Salmani et al. [70] rearrange scan chains to increase the detection of hardware Trojans. The appliance used to test integrated circuits is usually not bound to a specific layout on the chip. The approach suggests a layout that rearranges scan chains over the entire chip area so that certain areas can be specifically activated or deactivated during the functional test (see Figure 4.1). This should make the activity of a Trojan visible. Experimental tests show a partial amplification of Trojan activity by a factor of 30. In the industry, the very similar *physical scan chain reordering* is also used to minimize routing resources.

Tehranipoor et al. [77] highlight existing approaches for the detection of hardware Trojans and derive important paradigms for future research. They find that, so far, there are no benchmark tests available that can efficiently evaluate the effectiveness of countermeasures. Furthermore, there are no development platforms available to verify the approaches with the help of hardware. Such platforms are necessary, mainly because the commonly used FPGA systems are only of limited usefulness. For example, they cannot be used to perform transient analysis. To compare the effectiveness of the different measures, metrics for Trojan detection must be developed. The authors state that the *golden reference chips* (golden model), which are often taken as a basis and used for side-channel analysis to detect Trojans, should be replaced by more robust methods of comparison. In order to be able to ensure confidence in the hardware, policies and strategies for Design for Hardware Trust (DHT) should be developed and applied. They also consider developing trust in COTS and teaching the aspects of hardware security essential.

An overview of the topic of hardware Trojans is supplied by Tehranipoor and Sunar [78]. Their work starts by formulating the *Untrusted Manufacturer Problem*. It states that the design process is trusted until the tape-out. After the tape-out, the production process is no longer trusted. In addition to Trojans and their components, they discuss approaches for detecting and preventing hardware Trojan attacks.

Waksman and Sethumadhavan [81] present an approach to combat Trojans especially in microprocessors at runtime. However, in contrast to Tehranipoor and Sunar [78], in their paper the design process is not trusted: they address the possibility that malicious functionality is injected during the design phase by malicious designers. The following constraints are defined: 1. the number of malicious designers is low; 2. the activity of malicious designers remains unnoticed; 3. the attackers need few resources to inject a backdoor; 4. the backdoor is activated by a trigger; and 5. the Read-Only Memories (ROMs) written during the design phase contain correct data (microcode). Two types of backdoors serve as a Trojan model: *emitter* (send data) and *corruptor* (modify data) backdoors. The latter are very difficult to detect, since it can be hard to distinguish their operations from normal, legitimate operations. The measure proposed for preventing the hardware backdoors is an on-chip monitoring system that consists of four parts: predictor, reactor, target, and monitor (Figure 4.2(a)). Figure 4.2(b) shows details of the internal structure of the predictor and the monitor units.

The presence of a Trojan is assumed if the result of the monitored unit does not match the outcome predicted by the predictor. The detection principle is based on the assumption that the monitored unit never communicates with the monitoring instance—the designer of a malicious unit X therefore cannot corrupt the monitor of X.

Wei et al. [85] introduce a way of detecting Trojans using the method of GLC with thermal conditioning. Thermal conditioning means that an IC is intentionally heated unevenly. Here, the fact that the leakage power increases exponentially with temperature is exploited. The aim is to eliminate correlations when measuring leakage power that are caused by dependencies of gates with other gates (by heating correlated gates differently and thereby introducing more variability

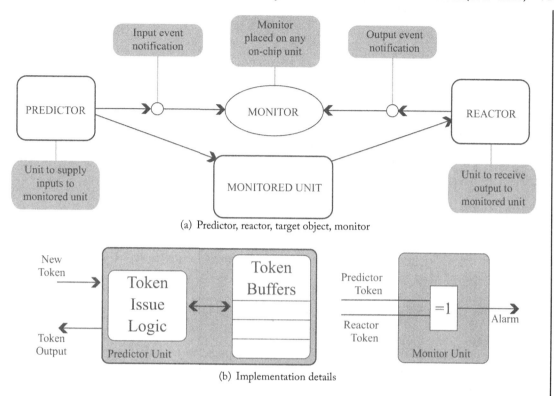

(a) Predictor, reactor, target object, monitor

(b) Implementation details

Figure 4.2: Principle of the monitoring system proposed by Waksman and Sethumadhavan [81].

to the calculation results). The entire process is calculated using a simulation model. First, the heat that will be generated per switch is determined for each gate. Meanwhile, the expected temperature for each unit of the IC is chosen for each gate and fed into a thermal model of the circuit to determine the necessary temperature for that specific gate. These specific gates are now heated exactly to the required temperature. By comparing the applied power to the calculated power, a statement can be made about the leakage power of a gate (see Figure 4.4). This then can be used to obtain scaling factors to calibrate the measurement procedure in order to minimize measurement variations caused by process variations. The advantage of applying this method is the full characterization of all gates of an IC. A linear program based on the GLC is solved for Trojan detection. An outcome close to 0 indicates a clean IC, otherwise it may have been modified (see Figure 4.3). The paper describes the mathematical foundations in much detail and in a reproducible way. Unfortunately, it lacks a concrete model for the investigated Trojans.

The detection of Trojans by GLC with thermal conditioning is not suitable for large circuits, because properties for the entire circuit are determined by GLC. Attackers can exploit this fact

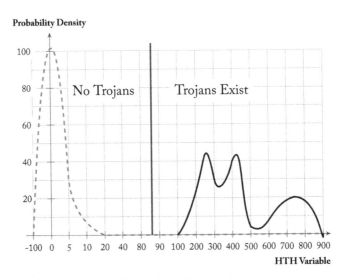

Figure 4.3: Variable for Trojan detection using thermal conditioning according to Wei et al. [85].

and inject ultra-small Trojans, whose impact will disappear in measurement noise (cf. Wei and Potkonjak [86]). To make the process scalable and thus useful for the analysis of large ICs, Wei and Potkonjak [86] expand the process by adding a preceding step of *segmentation*, which breaks up a large circuit into many small sub-circuits. The segmentation criteria are chosen in a way that ensures that the results of the subsequent GLC are as accurate as possible. The segmentation process itself is accomplished by varying a certain amount of primary input vectors and, at the same time, "freezing" the other input vectors. The circuit part obtained by segmentation is now seen as an independent part of the circuit (i.e., a *segment*). A GLC with thermal conditioning that is applied to this segment provides information about the potential presence of Trojan. A subsequent identification mechanism based on the principle of "guess and verify" then provides information about the type and the input pins of any existing Trojan. The output values do not overlap, so a clean threshold can be chosen (see Figure 4.3). Although the paper (cf. Wei and Potkonjak [86]) is very well written and explains complex relationships with a great degree of clarity, it makes no statement about the testing circuits that were used and the implemented Trojans (such as size, distribution, etc.). This circumstance makes it difficult to assess the practical usefulness of the procedure.

To demonstrate the vulnerability of hardware and to facilitate the development of hardware Trojans, a development platform is presented by Yun et al. [90]. The platform is designed as a PCI device. An FPGA serves as its core (see Figure 4.5(a)). Keyboard, temperature, and radio signals can be used as inputs. Serving as examples, three different hardware Trojans are implemented, where each of them use different trigger and payload mechanisms. Trojan 1 is triggered

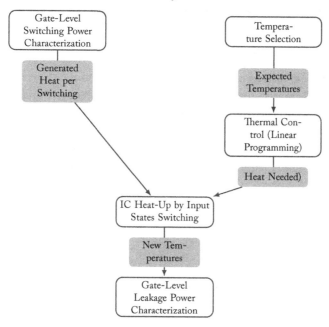

Figure 4.4: Detecting Trojans using GLC with thermal conditioning according to Wei et al. [85].

by exceeding the temperature of 100°C and blocks the PCI Bus. Trojan 2 is activated by typing a specific string on the keyboard and it overwrites the contents of an EEPROM (see Figure 4.5(b)). Trojan 3 is triggered by a specific radio signal and leaks confidential information. Although the paper has little scientific value, it still shows the need for development platforms to be able to purposefully create hardware Trojans.

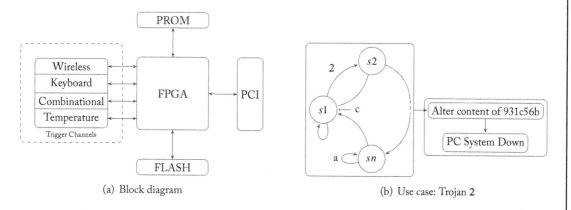

(a) Block diagram (b) Use case: Trojan 2

Figure 4.5: Development platform for hardware Trojans as introduced by Yun et al. [90].

4.3 A REFLECTION ON CURRENT APPROACHES (2011–2012)

A new class of attacks against cryptographic algorithms is presented by Ali et al. [5]. These so-called multi-level attacks rely on multiple persons involved in the hardware design and production process (see Figure 4.6(a)). The authors present an example of such an attack, where the secret key of a hardware implementation of the AES algorithm becomes recoverable by an inserted fault into the cipher text using known fault-attack techniques (see Figure 4.6(b)). The example assumes a link between the future malicious user and a corrupted developer who inserts the Trojan into the original circuit.

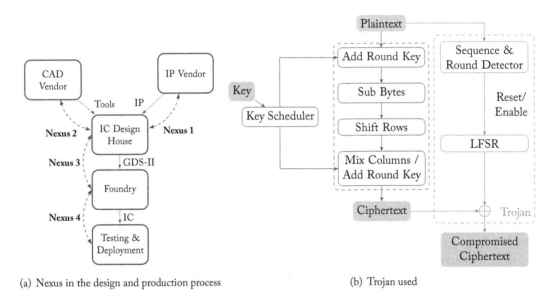

(a) Nexus in the design and production process   (b) Trojan used

Figure 4.6: Multi-level attack on an AES implementation proposed by Ali et al. [5].

A first approach for combining the characteristic possibilities of different methods of side-channel analysis is presented by Koushanfar and Mirhoseini [46], which is an advancement of their previous work (cf. Koushanfar et al. [47]). The framework allows analysis with different evaluation methods and by different side channels, such as the analysis of quiescent current, leakage current and delay (see Figure 4.7(a)). The mathematical analysis of the measurement results is based on a GLC and a subsequent statistical analysis. In this publication, a new objective function is defined for the linear program that takes into account the *submodularity* of the problem. Figure 4.7(b) visualizes the concept: The impact of a Trojan on a side channel grows when the observed area of the circuit is reduced. After the GLC, the deviation of the measurement results (obtained by the various side-channel analyses) from the expected values is calculated for each

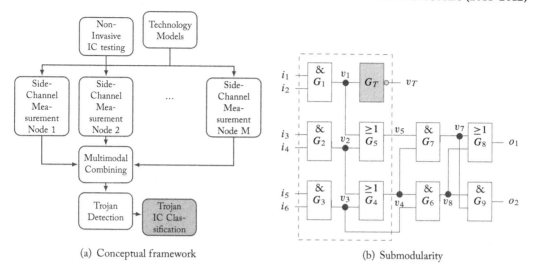

(a) Conceptual framework   (b) Submodularity

Figure 4.7: Multi-modal detection of Trojans according to Koushanfar and Mirhoseini [46].

gate. A sensitivity analysis is performed so that possible malicious circuits can be detected. The design of the Trojan determines the effect on the side channels. Some Trojans are more likely to have an impact on power consumption, while others will rather affect the performance. The measurement results of the different analyses (*multimodal*) are combined to achieve a higher detection rate. The authors' experiments provide up to 100% detection rates under some conditions. This method can also be used to predict areas of the design in which modifications are very difficult to find. Another contribution of this work is the introduction of a metric for assessing the suitability of different measuring methods based on their measurement sensitivity.

Lamech et al. [49] also evaluate the effectiveness of the combined results from the analyses of various side channels. In contrast to the work proposed by Koushanfar and Mirhoseini [46], however, no general model is presented in which the results of different side-channel analyses can be combined. The authors show that by using transient power and performance combined as side channels and analyzed with regression analysis, higher detection rates can be achieved in contrast to using each side channel on its own. They were able to achieve detection rates of up to 80% and boost it to up to 100% in their experiments. Figure 4.8(a) is a graphical representation of the regression analysis. The data points outside the confidence interval 3σ (green lines) are considered Trojans and marked red. It further shows that inter-chip process variations are random and thus have a rather small impact on the detection of Trojans. However, on-chip variations must be taken into account by calibrating because sometimes high variations (15%) can occur. Because, in practice, such a high resolution measurement of the delay can only be done with supporting infrastructure inside the chip itself, an approach is presented to convert the time into a digital

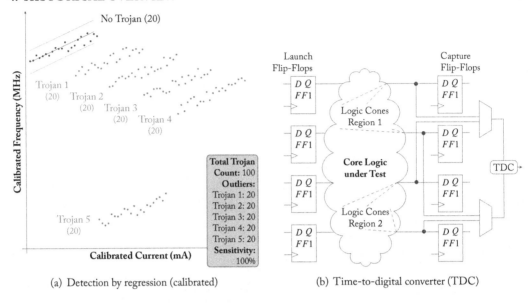

(a) Detection by regression (calibrated)   (b) Time-to-digital converter (TDC)

Figure 4.8: Detection by regression analysis and equipment for measuring delay with a high resolution based on Lamech et al. [49].

representation (Time-to-Digital-Converter (TDC), Figure 4.8(b)). A time interval is converted into thermometer code that corresponds to its digital representation.

To increase the probability of state transitions in circuits during functional tests, Salmani et al. present an approach in Salmani et al. [69, 71] that inserts dummy scan flip-flops into the original circuit layout. The consideration is that Trojans will be activated completely or in parts, and thereby have an impact on side channels. For example, gates of a Trojan might switch and the additional energy consumption could be visible in the course of a side-channel analysis. The biggest motivation is to shorten the authentication process of an IC. First, a threshold for the switching probability is determined that results from technical and economic considerations. Then, the switching probabilities of each sub-net are determined and the nets are divided into two groups, one with high and one with low switching probabilities. A dummy scan flip-flop is connected to nets with low switching probability to increase the probability of a transition. A net that tends to logic 0 is succeeded by a scan flip-flop that draws the output of the net (in a testing setup) to logic 1 if needed. The opposite is true for nets that tend to logic 1. Figure 4.9(a) shows such a scan flip-flop for nets that tend to be on logic 1. The highest probability for a transition exists if the probability for logic 1 and logic 0 are equal, i.e., 50% each. The switching probability is the product of the two probabilities; the maximum switching probability is, therefore, $50\% \cdot 50\% = 25\%$. It is interesting to note that there appears to be an optimum for the amount of inserted dummy scan flip-flops. In experimental tests, it was found that transitions in the entire circuit are reduced when switching probability is increased. As a result, large nets are harder to activate than small ones. This, in turn, means that the presented method is best suited for the detection of small Trojans. Figure 4.9(b) shows the ratio between the power consumed by the malicious circuits and the total power consumed, with and without dummy scan flip-flops. The power consumed by malicious circuits with dummy scan flip-flops is higher on average than without due to an increase in (partial) activation. Although the method presented here provides an interesting approach to the subject of activation increase, it must be noted that the attack model has an inherent error. The authors postulate that a Trojan is activated by the occurrence of a rare event. Therefore, the attacker in their model connects the Trojan to networks that are very hard to activate in order to avoid detection in functional tests. This requires extensive knowledge of the circuit design, which is probably only accessible to developers. However, the authors assume that the developers are trusted. Therefore, the attack takes place in the production phase, after the dummy scan flip-flops are inserted into the design. If an attacker wanted to connect the Trojan to networks that are rarely activated, this would require a comprehensive analysis of the existing production documents. This means that if an attacker is able to identify networks with low switching probability, she is also able to detect the inserted dummy scan flip-flops and can take steps to circumvent them. For this reason, the robustness of the proposed approach is assessed as low. If we assume that an attacker will insert malicious functionality during the development phase, this approach has no impact either, because a subsequent side-channel analysis has no "golden model" at hand (because the malicious circuit is already included).

Sturton et al. [75] research malicious circuits that the UCI approach given by Hicks et al. [32] does not detect and therefore classifies as benign. The method from Hicks et al. [32] is based on the assumption that Trojans are designed so that they do not activate at design time, and are therefore not used. This manifests itself in the fact that some of the inputs of unused circuits are always equal to the output and can therefore be replaced by a short circuit. Sturton et al. [75] now look for circuits that meet the conditions of the UCI but are malicious nonetheless. After introducing constraints (maximum number of gates, gate availability, maximum number of input-outputs, etc.), every possible combination of these gates is examined to determine whether this circuit is: 1. admissible, 2. obviously malicious, and 3. stealthy.

If a circuit meets these conditions, it can execute malicious functions and is still not recognized by UCI. Figure 4.10(a), for example, shows such an example circuit that, in the non-triggered state ($t_1 = t_0 = 0$), represents an AND gate ($f = i_0 \wedge i_1$). When it is in the triggered state ($t_1 = t_0 = 1$), it fulfills the function $f = i_0 \vee \neg i_1$. 4.10(b) shows the corresponding truth table. Experiments for a maximum of three gates, each with two inputs and one output, as well as a gate library of {AND,OR,NOT,NAND,2-input-MUX} for two trigger inputs and one or two non-trigger inputs yield 27 circuits with different Boolean functions from 256 possible ones. The authors further reported a decrease in detection rate the more test cases were checked by UCI. This phenomenon is explained by an increase in false negatives and a decrease in false positives. However, the more test cases are examined, the higher the risk that a Trojan is detected during a functional test. Therefore, attackers have to find the perfect balance between bypassing UCI and

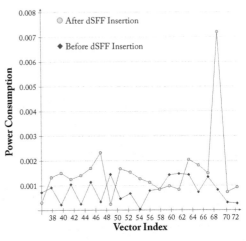

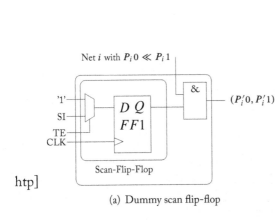

htp]

(a) Dummy scan flip-flop

(b) Power consumption with and without dummy scan flip-flops (side channel transient analysis)

Figure 4.9: Increase of the probability of transition via dummy scan flip-flops according to Salmani et al. [71].

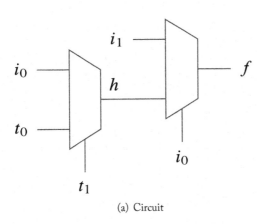

(a) Circuit

t_1	t_0	i_1	i_0	h	f	Comments
0	0	0	0	0	0	
0	0	0	1	1	0	$h \neq t_1, h \neq t_0, h \neq i_1$
0	0	1	0	0	0	
0	0	1	1	1	1	
0	1	0	0	0	0	
0	1	0	1	1	0	$f \neq t_0, f \neq i_0, f \neq h$
0	1	1	0	0	0	
0	1	1	1	1	1	
1	0	0	0	0	0	
1	0	0	1	0	0	$h \neq i_0$
1	0	1	0	0	0	$f \neq t_1, f \neq i_1$
1	0	1	1	0	1	
1	1	0	0	1	1	Trigger Condition is true
1	1	0	1	1	0	...
1	1	1	0	1	1	...
1	1	1	1	1	1	...

(b) Truth table

Figure 4.10: Example of a malicious circuit that is not detected by the UCI-method according to Sturton et al. [75].

staying hidden from functional tests. To still be able to test hardware for harmful components at design time, the authors propose to define a class of malicious circuits. One can search explicitly for such circuits in the course of a functional test. However, test methods that use test cases as their only specification for correct behavior (such as UCI) are not suited for this purpose, because the specification might be incomplete.

Waksman and Sethumadhavan [82] present an approach that is intended to prevent the occurrence of the trigger condition of digital, deterministic triggers (cf. Section 3.4.1). The authors first identify five types of interfaces within a digital system: 1. global, 2. control, 3. data, 4. test, and 5. output interfaces. Untrusted data is not monitored and manipulated within functional groups, but at their inputs and outputs. The idea is to scramble and obscure data in a controlled manner so that a trigger circuit cannot find a valid condition and, therefore, a Trojan will never get activated. The following types of triggers are considered: 1. ticking timebomb, 2. single-shot cheat code, and 3. sequence cheat code. A ticking timebomb is a time-controlled trigger that is activated when a predetermined number of clock cycles N has elapsed. The clock cycles that have already passed are usually determined using a counter. If this counter is always reset before reaching state N, a Trojan will never become active. This can be achieved by periodically resetting the entire digital system (*power reset*). The reset interval must be smaller than the testing period T that the obligatory functional test requires. If an attacker wants a ticking timebomb to be activated, this must occur within N clock cycles. However, if $N < T$, the Trojan will be activated and detected during the functional tests. Data-based triggers can be separated into single-shot cheat code and sequence cheat code triggers. Single-shot cheat code triggers are activated when a certain rare value is applied to the monitored interface. To prevent an attacker knowingly applying a rare value to an input of a compromised functional, it is obfuscated by shuffling so that it no longer meets the trigger condition. This approach is valid for non-computational units such as memory, etc. In order to protect computational units (e.g., Arithmetic Logical Unit (ALU)), *homomorphic* functions are used. Homomorphic functions obey the following rule: $f(g(x), g(y)) = g(f(x, y))$. An example of a homomorphic function is: $x^2 y^2 = (xy)^2$. If we assume that the computational function is squaring, a non-trustworthy value x that is to be processed is multiplied by a random value y before it is squared.

To obtain a valid result, the result at the output of the functional unit must be divided by y^2. The last class of triggers, sequence cheat codes, is countered by scrambling and inserting dummy loads. The scrambling is achieved by simple reordering. If this is not possible, dummy loads can be inserted into the data stream. A maximum number n of bits must be defined that is then allowed as a valid sequence. After n processed bits, a dummy load is inserted to avoid execution. A schematic representation of the proposed mechanisms is given in Figure 4.11(a). The authors evaluate their approach on a microprocessor whose source code is freely available, the OpenSPARC T2. Ticking timebombs are fought with the code implemented in Verilog in Figure 4.11(b). To combat data-based triggers, RAM and memory control are adapted slightly to scramble the sequence or to insert dummy loads. The authors show the that performance is

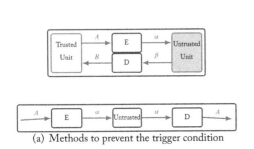

(a) Methods to prevent the trigger condition

```
module reset(clk, rst, out);
    input clk;
    input rst;
    output out;
    reg [19:0] countdown
    always @(posedge clk) begin
        if(rst) countdown <= 20'b0 -1'b1;
        else countdown <= countdown -1'b1;
    end
    assign out = (countdown == 0);
endmodule
```

(b) Exemplary implementation (Verilog) of the power reset method
according to Waksman and Sethumadhavan [82]

Figure 4.11: The Obfuscation approach proposed by Waksman and Sethumadhavan [82] to prevent hardware backdoors.

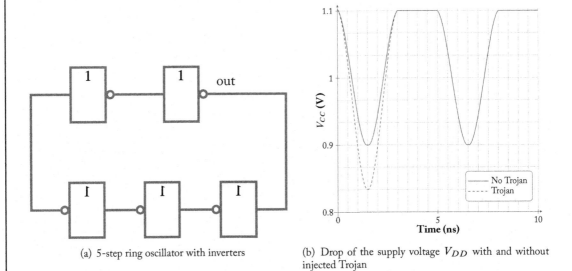

(a) 5-step ring oscillator with inverters

(b) Drop of the supply voltage V_{DD} with and without injected Trojan

Figure 4.12: Detection of Trojans using a network of ring oscillators (based on Zhang and Tehranipoor [92]).

affected at 1% on average with a maximum of 3.5% and that the methods can be used in modern microprocessors.

Zhang and Tehranipoor [92] use a network of ring oscillators to detect injected Trojans. A ring oscillator is a simple circuit for generating oscillations, consisting of an odd number of similar gates. Figure 4.12(a) shows such a circuit. The principle of detection is based on the fact that the frequency of a ring oscillator is influenced by a variety of physical parameters. Thus, the frequency also depends on the supply voltage V_{DD} (cf. Section 3.5 and Rajendran et al. [65]). When V_{DD} drops, the propagation delay increases and the cycle frequency drops. A slight drop of V_{DD} may occur near a current drawing gate.

In a CMOS gate, this is true for every state change. A possible Trojan might, therefore, influence adjacent ring oscillators with its activity. (see Figure 4.12(b)). To achieve the best possible coverage, ring oscillators are distributed over the entire chip area. Using statistical methods, in which the frequencies of the built-in ring oscillators are evaluated (simple outlier analysis, principal component analysis and advanced outlier analysis), the authors achieved a detection rate of up to 100% with their model of a Trojan. A similar evaluation using an FPGA provided detection rates between 80% and 100%. The robustness of the approach against direct attacks is considered to be very high because the manipulations have a direct impact on the frequency of the ring oscillators and, therefore, become visible immediately in functional tests.

CHAPTER 5

Hot Topics and Conclusions

5.1 HOT TOPICS IN HARDWARE SECURITY AND TRUST

This work shows that the issue of hardware Trojans has gained worldwide interest and that there are already numerous approaches for combating them. However, it also shows that the systematic study of the subject is still in an early stage. For example, there is, to date, no universal model for a Trojan from which the already proposed models could be derived as special cases. In light of this fact, we are planning to develop such a model in the near future.

Based on this model, we plan to develop metrics to be able to classify Trojans. It should be possible, among other things, to objectively evaluate the *complexity* of a malicious circuit. We also want to make the *impact* of an attack assessable using a *scale* that also needs to be developed. We, furthermore, plan to develop a comprehensive taxonomy of hardware Trojans.

Even though scientific research has shown that hardware Trojans are an emerging threat, there are very few publications on specific real-world scenarios. The reason for this is that the occurrence of malicious functionality in industrial products may have a negative impact on the image of a company. Future work will deal with this fact by developing hardware Trojan modeling kits to simulate different types of Trojans and to tests countermeasures in a more generic way (cf. Tehranipoor and Lee [76]). Events such as the Capture the Chip Contest during the Cyber-Security Awareness Week (*CSAW*) 2012 provide implementations of hardware Trojans that can serve as quasi-real world examples. In the near future, we expect similar more international oriented contests in the area of hardware Trojans. On trust–HUB [79] a collection of benchmarks is provided that can be used as a starting point for further investigations.

We showed that there are numerous approaches for detecting, locating and preventing Trojans. What is missing are the methods for *eliminating* the detected and localized malicious circuits as a defensive measure. Future research will also have to focus on this topic.

Furthermore, a certain level of trust has to be established within the hardware development life cycle to overcome the problems caused by decentralized production chains. Therefore, we are planning to introduce and evaluate models for a *secure* hardware development life cycle and to, furthermore, analyze its applicability in an industrial context.

Other hot topics in this area are:

- hardware architectures for cryptography

- trojan detection and isolation

- intellectual property protection and metering

- IC watermarking

- hardware security primitives (e.g., PUFs)

5.2   CONCLUSIONS

In this work, we presented a comprehensive survey of hardware Trojans and trust. Hardware Trojans are an emerging threat as the presence of designated hardware in different applications including household, financial and military systems continues to rise. Due to the high complexity of the hardware development life cycle and decentralized production chains, hardware becomes increasingly untrusted. In this book, we presented a brief introduction to the problem and gave a historical overview on hardware Trojans as well as the research conducted in this field in recent years. After introducing a taxonomy, we classified hardware Trojans according to their components and behavioral characteristics. Moreover, we provided countermeasures against malicious attacks on designated hardware and discussed their applicability in the context of hardware development. We also presented methodologies for the detection of hardware Trojans, such as formal verification, logic testing and side-channel analysis. We also introduced mechanisms to efficiently locate hardware Trojans within a system. We presented obfuscation and invasion as reliable ways of preventing hardware from being infected by hardware Trojans.

We carefully selected topologies and metrics introduced in state-of-the art scientific literature, giving a brief yet comprehensive introduction to hardware security and hardware Trojans, in particular.

Glossary

"On-Chip Variation" process variations on the same chip. These are naturally occurring production differences, such as thickness of layers or random dopant fluctuations, that influence the transistors performance. 75, 87, 88

1-to-Many Code One word of information will be copied to many words. 68

3D Hardware System Hardware system that has several connected layers on top of each other. 58

Activation Probablility Probability of a Trojan being activated during functional testing. 46

Address Decoder Circuit for decoding an binary address signal and activating the appropriate hardware component with one signal for each component. 59

AES The Advanced Encryption Standard (AES) is a symmetric encryption system established by the U.S. National Institute of Standards and Technology (NIST) in 2001. It is optimized for fast implementation in software and hardware. 25, 36, 68

ALU An Arithmetic Logical Unit (ALU) performs arithmetic and logic operations in a CPU. 79

ASIC An Application-Specific Integrated Circuit (ASIC) is an integrated circuit customized for a particular application, rather than intended for general purpose use. ix, 5, 16, 19, 20, 65

ATPG Automated Test Pattern Generation (ATPG) creates test patterns for Logic tests. 36

Backdoor Hidden access path to a (computer) system, usually with an elevated security level. 66, 70

Bus Arbiter Decides which bus participant gets access to the bus. 60

Bus Master The participant on the bus that initiates a bus transfer if the bus arbiter grants access. 59, 60

Bus Slave The participant on the bus that cannot access the bus unless requested by the bus master. 59, 60

CDMA Code Division Multiple Access (CDMA)is a modulation scheme where multiple users' data is encoded with different chipping sequences. The recipient requires the same sequence to decode the data. 14

COTS Commercial Off-The-Shelf (COTS). Typically, high volumes of such components lead to low prices. 70

CPLD Similar to FPGAs, Complex Programmable Logic Devices (CPLD) are cheaper and do not offer so many built-in functions. 20

CPU A Central Processing Unit (CPU) is responsible for running programs and processing data as described in that very program. See ALU. 61, 62

DARPA The Defense Advanced Research Projects Agency (DARPA; historically also ARPA, without *Defense*) is the research agency of the U.S. Department of Defense (DOD) which also funds many dual-use or civil projects. 65

Design Time The period in the design flow when the IC is developed. 58, 68

Detection Rate Ratio of Trojans that are detected in the IC in relation to all Trojans. 28, 29, 46, 66, 75, 77, 81

DHT Design for Hardware Trust (DHT). Rules for the design of ICs to verify the hardware. The fabrication is generally aided by extra hardware components. 70

DoS A Denial of Service (DoS) attack or condition prevents legitimate users or applications to access a service. 12, 60, 67

EEPROM Electrically Erasable and Programmable Read-Only Memory (EEPROM). A non-volatile re-writable memory which keeps its state without power. 73

EPLD Electrically Programmable Logic Device (EPLD) is an electronic component which function is defined after production, by programming it. See FPLA, CPLD, and FPGA. 20

Error Detection An error detection method can indicate various numbers of wrong bits, contingent on the transmission method. 68

False Negative The result of a probability test that indicates "false" although the correct result would be "true". 77

False Positive The result of a probability test that indicates "true" although the correct result would be "false". 77

Fan-Out Cone Amount of the parts of the circuit that are driven by the same output signal. 48

Flip-Flop Elementary memory cell in digital designs for holding one bit of information. 9, 23, 46, 48, 49, 67

Fmax, Maximum frequency, f_{max} Maximum frequency that can be used to drive an IC. 68

Formal Verification A formal method for showing the consistency of different representations (e.g., register-transfer level–system level). 23, 33, 68

FPGA A field-programmable gate array (FPGA) is an integrated circuit designed to be configured after manufacturing. It therefore contains versatile re-programmable logic blocks and a hierarchical interconnection network as well as some specialized function blocks (e.g., memory). Unlike CPLDs, logic functions are based on generic lookup-tables rather than real logic gates. ix, 5, 16, 20, 54, 65, 70, 72, 81

FPLA A Field-Programmable Logic Array (FPLA) is a early EPLD device, consisting only out of OR and AND gates. 20

Functional Test A functional verification procedure for determining the correct functionality of the whole circuit or parts of it. 8, 21, 23, 36, 37, 39, 40, 46, 47, 49, 54, 58, 67–69, 76, 77, 79, 81

Gate A gate represents a function from Boolean algebra (such as (N)OR, (N)AND, XOR,..). 14, 19, 23, 25, 35, 39, 46–48, 50, 52, 53, 66, 69, 75, 77, 81, 87

Gate Library Set of gates that can form a circuit. 77

Gate-level characterization The procedure of characterizing each single gate of a IC according to its physical (e.g., scaling factors) and manifestation (e.g., performance) properties. The approach is aimed at determining the effect of the Process variations, leading to more predictable characteristics of the gate level. xi, 39, 43, 50–52, 67, 69–74

Golden Model The golden model is accepted as free of malicious functionality and serves as reference. 17, 31, 35, 40, 49, 70

High-Level Synthesis The synthesizer tool compiles the high level description to register-transfer level. 20

IC Integrated Circuit (IC) is a set of electronic circuits on one small carrier plate. Such a circuit is typically much smaller than made from discrete independent components. 14, 16, 19–25, 33, 35, 45, 67, 68, 70–72, 76, 86–90

IDDT, Transient Current, I_{DDT} The current at transient transactions, i.e., switching of a gate. 33, 34, 36, 37, 41, 43, 51, 68

Inter-Chip Process Variation process variations between two chips. They are usually bigger than on-chip variations as different corners of the die are compared. 75, 88

Invasion Adding an extra part to an already existing circuit. x, 46, 58

Leakage Current Undesired flow of current through a transistor or integrated circuit. It occurs over closed transistors, insulators, or alternative paths. 39, 67, 74

Leakage Power Power dissipation caused by leakage current. 39, 69–71

Linear Program Linear programming is a way to determine the best solution for a given set of values that is described through linear equations and inequalities. 39, 71, 74

Logic Test Method for testing logical states by applying test input patterns and observing the outputs of each input pattern. 33, 34, 46, 66, 85

Malicious Circuit Circuitry added to a design with malicious intent. 23, 24, 41, 47, 53, 54, 66, 75, 77, 79, 83

Mask Masks are needed in the photolithography phase of the semiconductor fabrication. 21

Microcode Code in the ROM of a microprocessor that controls the state machine of the processor. Interface between hardware and software, sometimes called firmware. 70

Microprocessor Active hardware structure that can execute different commands. The main parts are: register, control unit, operation decoder, wire and cache. All parts are integrated on a microchip. 19, 70, 79, 80, 87

Mixed-Signal System Chip with analog and digital components. 18

MOLES Malicious Off-Chip Leakage Enabled by Side Channels. 67

Multi-Core System Integrated circuit with multiple processor cores. 55, 67

Netlist Representation of a hardware at a low level; consists of gates and its connectivity (wires). 33, 53

Non-Trigger Input The input is not a trigger for a Trojan. 77

Obfuscation A security procedure for hiding data or code parts. x, xi, 52, 55–57, 80

Outlier Analysis A (probabilistic) analysis of measurement data, identifies values in a predefined range. 45

    advanced Outlier analysis considers data from measurements and the correlation between the components. 44, 45, 81

    simple Outlier analysis considers data from many measurements. 45, 81

payload The core task of an active Trojan. ix, 7, 11–14, 72

Photolithography In the context of hardware development, photolithography is a process used in micro-fabrication to transfer geometric patterns to a light-sensitive chemical. Further chemical treatments then remove and deposit further materials, building up semiconductor structures layer by layer. 21, 87

Post-Silicon Period in the design flow of an ICs after its fabrication. 68

Pre-Silicon Period in the design flow of an ICs before its fabrication. 68

Principal Component Analysis Method for simplifying multivariable probabilistic systems through the linear combination of the principal components. x, 41, 42, 44, 45, 81

Process Variation The natural occurring variations in the manufacturing process (e.g., thickness of layers) and influence the parameters of the integrated circuit (e.g., speed) in fabrication. In practice, we differentiate between inter-chip process variation and on-chip variation, where the former is usually bigger, as parameters from different corners of the die are compared. 37, 39, 40, 49, 52, 67, 71, 85, 87

Propagation Delay The time elapsed between the input of a gate and the presence of a stable output. 35, 39, 81

Quiescent Current The current that is consumed by a circuit when it is not performing any work (also called standby current). 33, 74

Register-Transfer Level A level of abstraction in the design from ICs where the behavior is represented by registers and data flows first. 86, 87

Ring Oscillator A ring oscillator is a serial circuit of an odd number of gates with feedback on the input. The resulting frequency is a function of the number of gates, temperature, etc. x, xi, 18, 45, 51, 80, 81

ROM One-time programmable memory (Read-Only-Memory), typically filled during design time. 70

Root System user with all administrative rights on Unix and Unix-like systems. 66

Runtime The time when the hardware and software components are doing their tasks. 68, 70

Scan Chain Infrastructure inside an ICs for testing purposes during production. Scan flip-flops are connected to form a chain that allows the preloading of flops to stimulate combinatorial logic and to observe results. xi, 69

Scan Flip-Flop Flip-flop with additional circuitry for performing functional tests. xi, 21, 49, 67, 76–78, 89

Scheduler Arbiter of a multi-tasking system. 55

Segmentation Splitting a circuit into several partitions. 72

Sensitivity Term from measuring technology; describes the change in the output as the result of a change in the input. If a small input change leads to a considerable change in output, the system is more sensitive than if the output change was smaller. 69, 75

Side Channel Physical or logical parameter unintentionally modified as by-product of another task, not explicitly intended for the overall implementation. A side-channel attack is aimed at exploiting a side channel and receiving information about the processed data. ix, 33, 35, 36, 40, 41, 45, 51, 75, 76, 78

Side-Channel Analysis Analysis of physical parameters for their information content that were not intentionally made for information transmission. ix, 14, 16, 17, 21, 33–37, 40, 42, 45, 46, 48, 49, 51, 65–70, 74–76

Simulation A validation method where an abstract model of reality is executed in an observable environment. 33, 34, 40

SiP System-in-a-Package (SiP). A package contains multiple ICs that behave as a homogeneous hardware system. The ICs are connected to each other through different layers. 20

SNR Signal-to-noise ratio (SNR). The ratio between the actual signal and the background noise. It indicates the quality of the signal. 69

SoC System-on-a-Chip (SoC). A complete computer system integrated on a single chip. 20, 67

Spread-Spectrum The signal is transmitted at a higher bandwidth using a code sequence. 67

Standard Cell This part of the circuit is built on the electrical, logical, and physical properties from a library. 19

State Machine A finite state machine serves as a behavioral model. Its main parts are states, transitions, and actions. 53, 87

Structural Verification Examination of a structural description of a hardware component. 23, 65

Switching Power Dynamic power dissipation occurs through charging gate and wire capacitance whenever a gate is switched. 37, 39, 67, 69

System Description Language A programming language that describes a computer system on a high level of abstraction (e.g., SystemC, SystemVerilog). 20

System Level Highest level of abstraction at the design of ICs where the method of implementation is not specified. 86

Tape-Out In the fabrication process, tape-out designates the transfer of the designed circuit to the mask production and marks the turning point where the design phase ends and the physical production begins. (Named after the computer tapes used in former days). 16, 21, 23, 24, 33, 70, 90

Post- Time period after tape-out. 17

Pre- Time period before tape-out. 17

TDC A Time-to-Digital Converter (TDC) commonly measures a time interval and provide a binary output. 76

Test Pattern Bit flow to test the behavior of the ICs. 68, 69

Test Synthesis Phase of the design flow of the IC where deduced logic is included. Its purpose is to test the features and the constructed design. 21

Thermal Conditioning Uneven heating of a IC to characterize a logic circuit. xi, 70–73

Thermometer Code Also called *unary code*. A number is represented by an equivalent count of the digit one, e.g., decimal 5 = unary 11111. 76

TIC TRUST in Integrated Circuits. 65

Ticking Timebomb The payload of an attack is activated after a particular time period. 79

Toggle Flip between two excluding states, e.g., electrical *high* and *low*. 48, 66, 67

Transient Analysis Analysis method for measuring the response (voltage or current) to a step function. 69, 78

Transition Change from one state to another. Unlike *toggle*, not limited to two states. 76

Trigger A mechanism that activates a Trojan. ix, 7–10, 13, 14, 56, 58, 61, 70, 72, 79, 88, 90

Trigger Condition When the trigger condition is fulfilled, the Trojan becomes active. 10, 13, 14, 56, 57, 67, 68, 79, 80

Trigger Input The input is a trigger for a Trojan. 77

Trojan Also called *Trojan Horse* from Greek mythology. Non-self-replicating type of malware that pretends to be a useful device or function. ix–xi, 7–22, 24, 25, 31, 32, 34–37, 39–41, 43, 45, 46, 48, 49, 51–61, 66–77, 79–81, 83, 86, 88, 90

UCI Unused Circuit Identification (UCI) is a method for discovering Trojan circuits. xi, 58, 68, 77–79

Wafer Raw material for semiconductor fabrication used for the production of dies. 21

Bibliography

[1] AARESTAD, J., ACHARYYA, D., RAD, R., AND PLUSQUELLIC, J. 2010. Detecting Trojans Through Leakage Current Analysis Using Multiple Supply Pad IDDQs. In *Transactions on Information Forensics and Security*. Vol. 5. 893–904. DOI: 10.1109/TIFS.2010.2061228. x, 36, 41, 43

[2] ABRAMOVICI, M. AND BRADLEY, P. 2009. Integrated circuit security: new threats and solutions. In *CSIIRW '09: Proceedings of the 5th Annual Workshop on Cyber Security and Information Intelligence Research*. 1–3. DOI: 10.1145/1558607.1558671. x, 54, 55

[3] ADEE, S. 2008. The Hunt For The Kill Switch. In *IEEE Spectrum*. DOI: 10.1109/MSPEC.2008.4505310. 12, 66

[4] AGRAWAL, D., BAKTIR, S., KARAKOYUNLU, D., ROHATGI, P., AND SUNAR, B. 2007. Trojan Detection using IC Fingerprinting. In *SP '07: Proceedings of the IEEE Symposium on Security and Privacy*. 296–310. DOI: 10.1109/SP.2007.36. ix, 35, 40, 41, 65

[5] ALI, S. S., CHAKRABORTY, R. S., MUKHOPADHYAY, D., AND BHUNIA, S. 2011. Multi-level attacks: An emerging security concern for cryptographic hardware. In *DATE 2011: Proceedings of the Design, Automation & Test in Europe Conference & Exhibition*. 1–4. DOI: 10.1109/DATE.2011.5763307. xi, 23, 74

[6] ALKABANI, Y. AND KOUSHANFAR, F. 2008. Extended abstract: Designer's hardware Trojan horse. In *HOST 2008: Proceedings of the IEEE Internation Workshop on Hardware-Oriented Security and Trust*. 82–83. DOI: 10.1109/HST.2008.4559059. 23

[7] ALKABANI, Y. AND KOUSHANFAR, F. 2009. Consistency-based characterization for IC Trojan detection. In *ICCAD 2009: Proceedings of the 2009 International Conference on Computer-Aided Design*. 123–127. DOI: 10.1145/1687399.1687426. 17, 40

[8] ANDERSON, M. S., NORTH, C. J. G., AND YIU, K. K. 2008. Towards Countering the Rise of the Silicon Trojan. In *Technical Report by the Defence Science and Technology Organisation, Departement of Defence of the Australian Government*. 66

[9] BANGA, M. 2008. Partition based Approaches for the Isolation and Detection of Embedded Trojans in ICs. Master's Thesis, Virginia Polytechnic Institute. 35, 66

[10] BANGA, M. 2008. Testing and Verification Strategies for Enhancing Trust in Third Party IPs. Ph.D. Thesis, Virginia Polytechnic Institute. 14

[11] BANGA, M., CHANDRASEKAR, M., FANG, L., AND HSIAO, M. S. 2008. Guided Test Generation for Isolation and Detection of Embedded Trojans in ICs. In *GLSVLSI '08: Proceedings of the 18th ACM Great Lakes symposium on VLSI*. 363–366. DOI: 10.1145/1366110.1366196. 35, 48, 66

[12] BANGA, M. AND HSIAO, M. 2008. A region based approach for the identification of hardware Trojans. In *HOST 2008: Proceedings of the IEEE International Workshop on Hardware-Oriented Security and Trust*. 40–47. DOI: 10.1109/HST.2008.4559047. x, 17, 34, 40, 48, 49, 66

[13] BANGA, M. AND HSIAO, M. 2009. A Novel Sustained Vector Technique for the Detection of Hardware Trojans. In *VLSI Design 2009: 22nd International Conference on VLSI Design*. 327–332. DOI: 10.1109/VLSI.Design.2009.22. x, 17, 40, 49, 50, 66

[14] BANGA, M. AND HSIAO, M. 2009. VITAMIN: Voltage inversion technique to ascertain malicious insertions in ICs. In *HOST 2009: Proceedings of the IEEE International Workshop on Hardware-Oriented Security and Trust*. 104–107. DOI: 10.1109/HST.2009.5224960. 17, 40, 46, 66

[15] BANGA, M. AND HSIAO, M. S. 2010. Trusted RTL: Trojan detection methodology in pre-silicon designs. In *HOST 2010: Proceedings of the IEEE International Workshop on Hardware-Oriented Security and Trust*. 56–59. DOI: 10.1109/HST.2010.5513114. 68

[16] BANGA, M. AND HSIAO, M. S. 2011. ODETTE: A non-scan design-for-test methodology for Trojan detection in ICs. In *HOST 2011: Proceedings of the IEEE International Workshop on Hardware-Oriented Security and Trust*. 18–23. DOI: 10.1109/HST.2011.5954989. 54

[17] BAUMGARTEN, A., STEFFEN, M., CLAUSMAN, M., AND ZAMBRENO, J. 2010. A case study in hardware Trojan design and implementation. In *International Journal of Information Security*. Vol. 10. 1–14. DOI: 10.1007/s10207-010-0115-0. 22, 23, 66

[18] BLOOM, G., NARAHARI, B., SIMHA, R., AND ZAMBRENO, J. 2009. Providing secure execution environments with a last line of defense against Trojan circuit attacks. In *International Journal of Computers & Security*. Vol. 28. 660–669. DOI: 10.1016/j.cose.2009.03.002. x, 61, 62

[19] BLOOM, G., SIMHA, R., AND NARAHARI, B. 2009. OS support for detecting Trojan circuit attacks. In *HOST 2009: Proceedings of the IEEE International Workshop on Hardware-Oriented Security and Trust*. 100–103. DOI: 10.1109/HST.2009.5224959. x, 59, 60, 67

[20] CHAKRABORTY, R., NARASIMHAN, S., AND BHUNIA, S. 2009. Hardware Trojan: Threats and emerging solutions. In *HLDVT 2009: Proceedings of the IEEE International High Level Design Validation and Test Workshop*. 166–171. DOI: 10.1109/HLDVT.2009.5340158. ix, 7, 9, 10, 11, 12, 14, 31

[21] CHAKRABORTY, R., PAUL, S., AND BHUNIA, S. 2008. On-demand transparency for improving hardware Trojan detectability. In *HOST 2008: Proceedings of the IEEE International Workshop on Hardware-Oriented Security and Trust*. 48–50. DOI: 10.1109/HST.2008.4559048. x, 34, 46, 47, 53, 66

[22] CHAKRABORTY, R., WOLFF, F., PAUL, S., PAPACHRISTOU, C., AND BHUNIA, S. 2009. MERO: A Statistical Approach for Hardware Trojan Detection. In *CHES 2009: Proceedings of the International Workshop on Cryptographic Hardware and Embedded Systems*. 396–410. DOI: 10.1007/978-3-642-04138-9_28. 34, 66

[23] CHAKRABORTY, R. S. AND BHUNIA, S. 2008. Hardware protection and authentication through netlist level obfuscation. In *ICCAD 2008: Proceedings of the International Conference on Computer-Aided Design*. 674–677. DOI: 10.1109/ICCAD.2008.4681649. 53

[24] CHAKRABORTY, R. S. AND BHUNIA, S. 2009. Security against hardware Trojan through a novel application of design obfuscation. In *ICCAD 2009: Proceedings of the International Conference on Computer-Aided Design*. 113–116. DOI: 10.1145/1687399.1687424. x, 34, 53, 54

[25] CHAKRABORTY, R. S., SAHA, I., PALCHAUDHURI, A., AND NAIK, G. K. 2013. Hardware Trojan Insertion by Direct Modification of FPGA Configuration Bitstream. Vol. 30. 45–54. 5

[26] CHECKOWAY, S., MCCOY, D., KANTOR, B., ANDERSON, D., SHACHAM, H., SAVAGE, S., KOSCHER, K., CZESKIS, A., ROESNER, F., AND KOHNO, T. 2011. Comprehensive experimental analyses of automotive attack surfaces. In *USENIX 2011: Proceedings of the 20th USENIX conference on Security*. 1

[27] CHEN, Z., GUO, X., NAGESH, A., REDDY, M., AND MAITI, A. 2008. Hardware Trojan Designs on BASYS FPGA Board. Technical Report, Virginia Polytechnic Institute and State University. 66

[28] DARPA. 2007. Trust in Integrated circuits (TIC). Last accessed on: 2013-07-14. 65

[29] DAS, A., MEMIK, G., ZAMBRENO, J., AND CHOUDHARY, A. 2010. Detecting/preventing information leakage on the memory bus due to malicious hardware. In *DATE 2010: Proceedings of the Design, Automation Test in Europe Conference Exhibition*. 861–866. DOI: 10.1109/DATE.2010.5456930. x, 60, 61, 68

[30] DEFENSE SCIENCE BOARD, DEPARTMENT OF DEFENSE, U.S.. 2005. High Performance Microchip supply. Defence Sciene Board Report. ix, 5, 6, 7, 21, 65

[31] Du, D., Narasimhan, S., Chakraborty, R., and Bhunia, S. 2010. Self-referencing: A Scalable Side-Channel Approach for Hardware Trojan Detection. In *CHES 2010: Proceedings of the International Conference on Cryptographic Hardware and Embedded Systems.* 173–187. DOI: 10.1007/978-3-642-15031-9_12. 51, 68

[32] Hicks, M., Finnicum, M., King, S. T., Martin, M. M. K., and Smith, J. M. 2010. Overcoming an untrusted computing base: Detecting and removing malicious hardware automatically. In *SP 2010: Proceedings of the IEEE Symposium on Security and Privacy.* 159–172. DOI: 10.1109/SP.2010.18. x, 58, 59, 68, 77

[33] HOST. 2008. IEEE International Workshop on Hardware-Oriented Security and Trust – Final Program. 66

[34] HOST. 2009. 2nd IEEE International Workshop on Hardware-Oriented Security and Trust – Final Program. 68

[35] Huffmire, T., Valamehr, J., Sherwood, T., Kastner, R., Levin, T., Nguyen, T., and Irvine, C. 2008. Extended abstract: Trustworthy system security through 3-D integrated hardware. In *HOST 2008: Proceedings of the IEEE International Workshop on Hardware-Oriented Security and Trust.* 91–92. DOI: 10.1109/HST.2008.4559061. 58, 66

[36] Jha, S. and Jha, S. 2008. Randomization based probabilistic approach to detect Trojan circuits. In *HASE 2008: Proceedings of the High Assurance Systems Engineering Symposium.* 117–124. DOI: 10.1109/HASE.2008.37. 23, 66

[37] Jin, Y. and Makris, Y. 2008. Hardware Trojan detection using path delay fingerprint. In *HOST 2008: Proceedings of the IEEE International Workshop on Hardware-Oriented Security and Trust.* 51–57. DOI: 10.1109/HST.2008.4559049. 17, 35, 37, 40, 66

[38] Jin, Y. and Makris, Y. 2010. Hardware Trojans in wireless cryptographic ICs. In *IEEE Journal of Design Test of Computers.* Vol. 27. 26–35. DOI: 10.1109/MDT.2010.21. x, 12, 14, 18, 25, 36, 40, 42, 68

[39] Karri, R., Rajendran, J., Rosenfeld, K., and Tehranipoor, M. 2010. Trustworthy hardware: Identifying and classifying hardware Trojans. In *IEEE Journal Computer.* Vol. 43. 39–46. DOI: 10.1109/MC.2010.299. 68

[40] Kean, T., McLaren, D., and Marsh, C. 2008. Verifying the authenticity of chip designs with the DesignTag system. In *HOST 2008: Proceedings of the IEEE International Workshop on Hardware-Oriented Security and Trust.* 59–64. DOI: 10.1109/HST.2008.4559051. 18, 35, 45

[41] Keren, O., Levin, I., and Karpovsky, M. 2010. Duplication based one-to-many coding for Trojan HW detection. In *DFT 2010: Proceedings of the IEEE International Symposium on*

Defect and Fault Tolerance in VLSI Systems (DFT). 160–166. DOI: 10.1109/DFT.2010.26. 68

[42] KIM, L.-W., VILLASENOR, J., AND KOC, C. 2009. A Trojan-resistant system-on-chip bus architecture. In *MILCOM 2009: Proceedings of the IEEE Conference on Military Communications*. 1–6. DOI: 10.1109/MILCOM.2009.5379966. 59, 67

[43] KIM, L.-W. AND VILLASENOR, J. D. 2010. A system-on-chip bus architecture for thwarting integrated circuit Trojan horses. In *IEEE Transactions on Very Large Scale Integration (VLSI) Systems*. Vol. 19. 1921–1926. DOI: 10.1109/TVLSI.2010.2060375. 59

[44] KING, S. AND CHEN, P. 2006. SubVirt: implementing malware with virtual machines. In *SP 2006: Proceedings of the IEEE Symposium on Security and Privacy*. 314–327. DOI: 10.1109/SP.2006.38. 2

[45] KING, S. T., TUCEK, J., COZZIE, A., GRIER, C., JIANG, W., AND ZHOU, Y. 2008. Designing and implementing malicious hardware. In *LEET 2008: Proceedings of the 1st Usenix Workshop on Large-Scale Exploits and Emergent Threats*. 1–8. 25, 66

[46] KOUSHANFAR, F. AND MIRHOSEINI, A. 2011. A unified framework for multimodal submodular integrated circuits Trojan detection. In *IEEE Transactions on Information Forensics and Security*. Vol. 6. 162–174. DOI: 10.1109/TIFS.2010.2096811. xi, 35, 36, 37, 39, 52, 74, 75

[47] KOUSHANFAR, F., MIRHOSEINI, A., AND ALKABANI, Y. 2010. A unified submodular framework for multimodal IC Trojan detection. In *IH 2010: Proceedings of the Conference on Information Hiding*, R. Böhme and P. Fong, and R. Safavi-Naini, Ed. 69, 74

[48] KUHN, M. 2008. Trojan hardware – some strategies and defenses. Lecture Notes, Schloss Dagstuhl 2008. 23

[49] LAMECH, C., RAD, R., TEHRANI, M., AND PLUSQUELLIC, J. 2011. An experimental analysis of power and delay signal-to-noise requirements for detecting Trojans and methods for achieving the required detection sensitivities. In *IEEE Transactions on Information Forensics and Security*. Vol. 6. 1170–1179. DOI: 10.1109/TIFS.2011.2136339. xi, 35, 36, 37, 41, 45, 75, 76

[50] LI, J. AND LACH, J. 2008. At-speed delay characterization for IC authentication and Trojan Horse detection. In *HOST 2008: Proceedings of the IEEE International Workshop on Hardware-Oriented Security and Trust*. 8–14. DOI: 10.1109/HST.2008.4559038. 17, 35, 37, 40, 45, 66

[51] LIN, L., BURLESON, W., AND PAAR, C. 2009. MOLES: Malicious off-chip leakage enabled by side-channels. In *ICCAD 2009: Proceedings of the International Conference on Computer-Aided Design*. 117–122. DOI: 10.1145/1687399.1687425. 67

[52] LIN, L., KASPER, M., GÜNEYSU, T., PAAR, C., AND BURLESON, W. 2009. Trojan side-channels: Lightweight hardware Trojans through side-channel engineering. In *CHES 2009: Proceedings of the Conference on Cryptographic Hardware and Embedded Systems*. 5747. DOI: 10.1007/978-3-642-04138-9_27. 12, 14, 67

[53] MCINTYRE, D., WOLFF, F., PAPACHRISTOU, C., AND BHUNIA, S. 2010. Trustworthy computing in a multi-core system using distributed scheduling. In *IOLTS 2010: Proceedings of the IEEE Symposium on On-Line Testing*. 211–213. DOI: 10.1109/IOLTS.2010.5560200. x, 55, 56

[54] MCLNTYRE, D., WOLFF, F., PAPACHRISTOU, C., BHUNIA, S., AND WEYER, D. 2009. Dynamic evaluation of hardware trust. In *HOST 2009: Proceedings of the IEEE International Workshop on Hardware-Oriented Security and Trust*. 108–111. DOI: 10.1109/HST.2009.5224990. 55, 67

[55] NARASIMHAN, S. AND BHUNIA, S. 2012. Hardware Trojan detection. In *Introduction to Hardware Security and Trust*, M. Tehranipoor and C. Wang, Eds. Springer New York, 339–364. 33

[56] NARASIMHAN, S., DU, D., CHAKRABORTY, R., PAUL, S., WOLFF, F., PAPACHRISTOU, C., ROY, K., AND BHUNIA, S. 2010. Multiple-parameter side-channel analysis: A non-invasive hardware Trojan detection approach. In *HOST 2010: Proceedings of the IEEE International Workshop on Hardware-Oriented Security and Trust*. 13–18. DOI: 10.1109/HST.2010.5513122. 34, 68

[57] NELSON, M., NAHAPETIAN, A., KOUSHANFAR, F., AND POTKONJAK, M. 2009. SVD-based ghost circuitry detection. In *Lecture Notes on Information Hiding*. 5806. DOI: 10.1007/978-3-642-04431-1_16. 17, 39, 43, 67

[58] POTKONJAK, M. 2010. Synthesis of trustable ICs using untrusted CAD tools. In *DAC 2010: Proceedings of the 47th Conference on Design Automation Conference*. 633–634. DOI: 10.1145/1837274.1837435. 17

[59] POTKONJAK, M., NAHAPETIAN, A., NELSON, M., AND MASSEY, T. 2009. Hardware Trojan horse detection using gate-level characterization. In *DAC 2009: Proceedings of the 46th Conference on Design Automation*. 688–693. DOI: 10.1145/1629911.1630091. 17, 39, 40, 67

[60] RAD, R., PLUSQUELLIC, J., AND TEHRANIPOOR, M. 2008. Sensitivity analysis to hardware Trojans using power supply transient signals. In *HOST 2008: Proceedings of the IEEE International Workshop on Hardware-Oriented Security and Trust*. 3–7. DOI: 10.1109/HST.2008.4559037. 36, 37, 66

[61] RAD, R., PLUSQUELLIC, J., AND TEHRANIPOOR, M. 2010. A sensitivity analysis of power signal methods for detecting hardware Trojans under real process and environmental conditions. In *IEEE Transactions on Very Large Scale Integration (VLSI) Systems*. DOI: 10.1109/TVLSI.2009.2029117. 36, 37, 69

[62] RAD, R., WANG, X., TEHRANIPOOR, M., AND PLUSQUELLIC, J. 2008. Power supply signal calibration techniques for improving detection resolution to hardware Trojans. In *ICCAD 2008: Proceedings of the International Conference on Computer-Aided Design*. 632–639. DOI: 10.1109/ICCAD.2008.4681643. ix, x, 14, 15, 17, 36, 37, 38, 40, 43, 51, 66

[63] RAI, D. AND LACH, J. 2009. Performance of delay-based Trojan detection techniques under parameter variations. In *HOST 2009: Proceedings of the IEEE International Workshop on Hardware-Oriented Security and Trust*. 58–65. DOI: 10.1109/HST.2009.5224966. 35, 37

[64] RAJENDRAN, J., GAVAS, E., JIMENEZ, J., PADMAN, V., AND KARRI, R. 2010. Towards a comprehensive and systematic classification of hardware Trojans. In *ISCAS 2010: Proceedings of the International Symposium on Circuits and Systems*. 1871–1874. DOI: 10.1109/IS-CAS.2010.5537869. 68

[65] RAJENDRAN, J., JYOTHI, V., AND KARRI, R. 2011. Blue team red team approach to hardware trust assessment. In *ICCD 2011: Proceedings of the International Conference on Computer Design*. 285–288. DOI: 10.1109/ICCD.2011.6081410. 63, 81

[66] RECONFIGURABLE COMPUTING FOR SECURITY AND CRYPTOGRAPHY. 2009. Call for papers - special track: Reconfigurable computing for security and cryptography. 68

[67] RILLING, J., GRAZIANO, D., HITCHCOCK, J., MEYER, T., WANG, X., JONES, P., AND ZAMBRENO, J. 2011. Circumventing a ring oscillator approach to FPGA-based hardware Trojan detection. In *ICCD 2011: Proceedings of the International Conference on Computer Design*. DOI: 10.1109/ICCD.2011.6081411. 40, 63

[68] ROY, J. A., KOUSHANFAR, F., AND MARKOV, I. L. 2008. Extended abstract: Circuit CAD tools as a security threat. In *HOST 2008: Proceedings of the IEEE International Workshop on Hardware-Oriented Security and Trust*. 65–66. DOI: 10.1109/HST.2008.4559052. 17, 23

[69] SALMANI, H., TEHRANIPOOR, M., AND PLUSQUELLIC, J. 2009. New design strategy for improving hardware Trojan detection and reducing Trojan activation time. In *HOST 2009: Proceedings of the IEEE International Workshop on Hardware-Oriented Security and Trust*. 66–73. DOI: 10.1109/HST.2009.5224968. 67, 76

[70] SALMANI, H., TEHRANIPOOR, M., AND PLUSQUELLIC, J. 2010. A layout-aware approach for improving localized switching to detect hardware Trojans in integrated circuits. In *WIFS 2010: Proceedings of the International Workshop on Information Forensics and Security*. 1–6. DOI: 10.1109/WIFS.2010.5711438. xi, 49, 69

[71] SALMANI, H., TEHRANIPOOR, M., AND PLUSQUELLIC, J. 2011. A novel technique for improving hardware Trojan detection and reducing Trojan activation time. In *IEEE Transactions on Very Large Scale Integration (VLSI) Systems.* DOI: 10.1109/TVLSI.2010.2093547. xi, 46, 76, 78

[72] SHARKEY, B. 2007. Briefing to industry. ix, 4, 5

[73] SMITH, S. AND DI, J. 2007. Detecting malicious logic through structural checking. In *IEEE Region 5 2007: Proceedings of the Region 5 Technical Conference.* 217–222. DOI: 10.1109/TPSD.2007.4380384. 33, 65

[74] SREEDHAR, A., KUNDU, S., AND KOREN, I. 2012. On reliability trojan injection and detection. *Journal on Low Power Electronics 8,* 5, 674–683. DOI: 10.1166/jolpe.2012.1225. 34

[75] STURTON, C., HICKS, M., WAGNER, D., AND KING, S. T. 2011. Defeating UCI: Building stealthy and malicious hardware. In *SP 2011: Proceedings of the International Symposium on Security and Privacy.* 64–77. DOI: 10.1109/SP.2011.32. xi, 23, 58, 77, 78

[76] TEHRANIPOOR, M. AND LEE, J. 2012. Protecting ips against scan-based side-channel attacks. In *Introduction to Hardware Security and Trust,* M. Tehranipoor and C. Wang, Eds. Springer New York, 411–427. 4, 12, 66, 83

[77] TEHRANIPOOR, M., SALMANI, H., ZHANG, X., WANG, M., KARRI, R., RAJENDRAN, J., AND ROSENFELD, K. 2010. Roadmap for trusted hardware – Part II: Trojan detection solutions and design-for-trust challenges. 70

[78] TEHRANIPOOR, M. AND SUNAR, B. 2010. Hardware Trojan horses. In *Towards Hardware-Intrinsic Security, D. Basin, U. Maurer, A.-R. Sadeghi, and D. Naccache.* 167–187. DOI: 10.1007/978-3-642-14452-3_7. 70

[79] TRUST–HUB. 2013. trust HUB Benchmarks. available at: `https://trusthub.engr. uconn.edu/resources/benchmarks`, last accessed on 2013-08-05. 83

[80] UNSAL, O. S., TSCHANZ, J. W., BOWMAN, K., DE, V., VERA, X., GONZALEZ, A., AND ERGIN, O. 2006. Impact of parameter variations on circuits and microarchitecture. DOI: 10.1109/MM.2006.122. 37

[81] WAKSMAN, A. AND SETHUMADHAVAN, S. 2010. Tamper evident microprocessors. In *SP 2010: Proceedings of the International Symposium on Security and Privacy.* 173–188. DOI: 10.1109/SP.2010.19. xi, 61, 70, 71

[82] WAKSMAN, A. AND SETHUMADHAVAN, S. 2011. Silencing hardware backdoors. In *SP 2011: Proceedings of the International Symposium on Security and Privacy.* 49–63. DOI: 10.1109/SP.2011.27. x, xi, 34, 56, 57, 61, 79, 80

[83] WANG, X., SALMANI, H., TEHRANIPOOR, M., AND PLUSQUELLIC, J. 2008. Hardware Trojan detection and isolation using current integration and localized current analysis. In *DFTVS 2008: Proceedings of the International Symposium on Defect and Fault Tolerance of VLSI Systems*. 87–95. DOI: 10.1109/DFT.2008.61. 17, 36, 40, 66

[84] WANG, X., TEHRANIPOOR, M., AND PLUSQUELLIC, J. 2008. Detecting malicious inclusions in secure hardware: Challenges and solutions. In *HOST 2008: Proceedings of the IEEE International Workshop on Hardware-Oriented Security and Trust*. 15–19. DOI: 10.1109/HST.2008.4559039. 66

[85] WEI, S., MEGUERDICHIAN, S., AND POTKONJAK, M. 2010. Gate-level characterization: Foundations and hardware security applications. In *DAC 2010: Proceedings of the 47th Conference on Design Automation*. 222–227. DOI: 10.1145/1837274.1837332. xi, 37, 39, 50, 70, 72, 73

[86] WEI, S. AND POTKONJAK, M. 2010. Scalable segmentation-based malicious circuitry detection and diagnosis. In *ICCAD 2010: Proceedings of the International Conference on Computer-Aided Design*. 483–486. DOI: 10.1109/ICCAD.2010.5653770. 72

[87] WOLFF, F., PAPACHRISTOU, C., BHUNIA, S., AND CHAKRABORTY, R. 2008. Towards Trojan-free trusted ICs: Problem analysis and detection scheme. In *DATE 2008: Proceedings of the European Conference on Design, Automation and Test*. 1362–1365. DOI: 10.1109/DATE.2008.4484928. 7, 11, 17, 25, 66

[88] WORKSHOP ON CRYPTOGRAPHIC HARDWARE AND EMBEDDED SYSTEMS 2009. 2009. Call for submissions – Hot topic session – Hardware Trojans and trusted ICs. 68

[89] YIN, C.-E. D., GU, J., AND QU, G. 2009. Hardware Trojan attack and hardening final report. Final Report of the CSAW 2009 Embedded System Challenges. x, 63, 64

[90] YUN, S., LI, Q., GAO, H., AND PING, Z. 2010. Towards hardware Trojan: Problem analysis and Trojan simulation. In *ICIES 2010: Proceedings of the International Conference on Information Engineering and Computer Science*. 1–4. DOI: 10.1109/ICIECS.2010.5677742. xi, 72, 73

[91] ZHANG, X. AND TEHRANIPOOR, M. 2011. Case study: Detecting hardware Trojans in third-party digital IP cores. In *HOST 2011: Proceedings of the IEEE Hardware-Oriented Security and Trust Symposium*. 67–70. DOI: 10.1109/HST.2011.5954998. 31, 33

[92] ZHANG, X. AND TEHRANIPOOR, M. 2011. RON: An on-chip ring oscillator network for hardware Trojan detection. In *DATE 2011: Proceedings of the European Conference on Design, Automation and Test*. 1–6. DOI: 10.1109/DATE.2011.5763260. x, xi, 36, 44, 45, 51, 80, 81

[93] KRIEG, C. AND WEIPPL, E. 2013. Malware in Hardware Infrastructure Components. In *Advances in IT Early Warning.* 65

Authors' Biographies

CHRISTIAN KRIEG

His research interests include hardware security, wireless sensor networks, and the Internet of Things.

Christian Krieg graduated with a Master's degree from Vienna University of Technology in 2013. After researching in the field of malicious hardware, he is now engaged at the Institute of Computer Technology in the detection and prevention of hardware Trojans using formal methods.

ADRIAN DABROWSKI

His research interests cover RFID, cyberphysical security, and hardware security.

Adrian Dabrowski received his Master's degree from Vienna University of Technology. He participated and later organized the Viennese iCTF team, winning two times. Before that he made several media appearances concerning insecurity of systems in public use and taught part-time at a technical high school.

HEIDELINDE HOBEL

Her research interests include, among others, software protection, privacy-preserving technologies and privacy by design.

She received a Master's degree in Business Informatics with focus on IT security from the Vienna University of Technology in 2013.

KATHARINA KROMBHOLZ

Her research interests include web 2.0 privacy and security, social networks, social engineering, hardware security, machine learning, human-computer interaction, and interaction design.

She received a Master's degree in Media Informatics from the Vienna University of Technology in 2012 and started her Ph.D in October 2013.

EDGAR WEIPPL

His research focuses on applied concepts of IT-security and e-learning.

After graduating with a Ph.D. from the Vienna University of Technology, Edgar worked in a research startup for two years. He then spent one year teaching as an assistant professor at Beloit College, WI. From 2002–2004, while with the software vendor ISIS Papyrus, he worked as a consultant in New York, NY and Albany, NY, and in Frankfurt, Germany. In 2004 he joined the Vienna University of Technology and founded the research center SBA Research together with A Min Tjoa and Markus Klemen.

Edgar R. Weippl (CISSP, CISA, CISM, CRISC, CSSLP, CMC) is member of the editorial board of *Computers & Security* (http://ees.elsevier.com/cose/COSE) and he organizes the ARES conference http://www.ares-conference.eu/conf/.

Printed in the United States
by Baker & Taylor Publisher Services